THE ✤ BOSTON
CELTICS

THE ✤ BOSTON CELTICS

JACK CLARY

Published by World Publications Group, Inc.
140 Laurel Street
East Bridgewater, MA 02333
www.wrldpub.net

ISBN 1-57215-331-8
978-1-57215-331-8

Printed and bound in China by SNP Leefung
Printers Limited.

1 2 3 4 5   06 05 03 02

PICTURE CREDITS

All photographs courtesy of UPI/Bettmann News
except the following:

AFP/Getty Images: page 89(right), 96(bottom).
Allsport/Rick Stewart: page 72.
Getty Images: pages 80(left), 82(top), 85, 92(left),
    95(top), 97(right).
Malcolm Emmons: pages 8(both), 33(bottom),
    49(bottom right), 50(both), 51(both), 52(both),
    53(both), 54, 55, 56(bottom left), 57, 58, 59(top),
    60(both), 62(both), 63, 70(bottom right), 71(both).
Nancy Hogue: pages 2, 56(bottom right), 61, 65(top),
    66, 67(both), 68(both).
Naismith Memorial Basketball Hall of Fame/The
    Edward J. and Gena G. Hickox Library: pages 11,
    13(bottom), 16, 17(bottom right), 21, 22(bottom
    right), 26(bottom), 29, 66(bottom left).
NBAE/Getty Images: pages 2, 3, 6(both), 8(top),
    9(bottom), 78, 79, 80(right), 81(both), 82(bottom),
    83(bottom), 84(both), 86, 88, 89(left), 91(both),
    92(right), 93, 94(both), 95(bottom), 96(top),
    97(left).
Bruce Schwartzman: pages 6(both), 7, 46(top),
    72(top right), 74, 75, 76, 77.
Brian Snyder/Reuters/Corbis: page 87.
Sports Illustrated/Getty Images: page 90.

ACKNOWLEDGMENTS

The author acknowledges the cooperation of the
Boston Celtics in assisting with this project, and
John Roman who did extensive legwork in ferreting
out needed information. Published works by three
good friends from the Boston media, Joe Fitzgerald,
George Sullivan and Bob Ryan, also proved to
be valuable resources that complemented all the
information I accumulated as a sports writer who
covered the NBA while working in New York and
Boston for 17 years; and which was enhanced over
the last 35 years as a freelance author of several
books about pro basketball.

DEDICATION

To the tens of thousands of Celtics adherents like myself
who became enamored with the team in the mid-fifties and
celebrated their great seasons of excellence that produced
all of those NBA championship banners which hang "high
above courtside," to quote the late, great announcer Johnny
Most. Chief among them is the greatest fan of all, my wife
Pat, and nephew J.T. Roman who came late to the show but
has been no less interested, in good times and bad.

Page 1: *Player-coach Bill
Russell faces the camera as
the Celtics take time out in the
waning moments of the fourth
playoff game with the 76ers
in 1967.*

Page 2: *Paul Pierce goes for
one of his many baskets in
Game 2 of the 2008 Finals
against the Lakers.*

Page 3: *Coach Doc Rivers
discusses some plays with Paul
Pierce and Rajon Rondo in
Game 4 of the playoffs against
Cleveland.*

Below: *Coach Red Auerbach
(far left) gets involved in a 1958
game. To his left is trainer Buddy
Leroux, who later became a part
owner of the Boston Red Sox.*

Contents

Preface

Below left: *Kevin Garnett makes a shot against the Lakers' Derek Fisher (#2) and Kobe Bryant (#24) in Game 6 of the 2008 Finals.*

Below right: *Ray Allen makes one of his baskets against the Lakers in the 6th and final game for the 2008 NBA Championship.*

Normalcy has returned to Boston. The Celtics once again ruled the National Basketball Association after winning the league's 2008 season title.

Twenty-two years had passed since championship banner No. 16 was lofted to the rafters in old Boston Garden, that grand arena that now exists only in the memories of 20th century Celtics fans and on the front of dog-eared memorabilia, and hanging a 17th championship banner in the TD Banknorth Garden (that's okay—you can still call it Boston Garden).

The time that it took to hang all of those original 16 championship banners was two

years less than it took to get No. 17. The accomplishment still felt the same because it was achieved with much of the style and tradition that were championship hallmarks of three distinct eras ruled by Bill Russell, John Havlicek and Larry Bird, the leaders of those great Celtics dynasties.

The newest flag was the product of hard work from a team led by Paul Pierce, one of the most talented players in the team's history. For nine seasons Pierce had paid his entry dues by excelling with mostly mediocre Celtics teams. But in 2007 he was joined by another talented forward named Kevin Garnett who had spent a dozen years

Left: *Kevin McHale (#32) and Reggie Lewis (#35) proved to be a great mix of old and new that continued the Celtics' success in 1991. McHale, a perennial all-pro forward, filled the famed "sixth man" role after playing on three Celtics NBA championship teams during the 1980s. Tragically, Lewis, a number one draft pick from Northeastern University in Boston, died from a heart attack in July 1993.*

playing for the Minnesota Timberwolves, searching in vain for a path to a championship. Along the way, they were joined by a smooth, pure-shooting guard named Ray Allen, who once played for the University of Connecticut and who had unflappable court presence. Finally, the Celtics had a clear path back to a championship.

They were led by head coach Glenn (Doc) Rivers whose greatest attribute was his ability to convince a team, half of whom had never played together until the 2007 season, to unite under his leadership and guidance and play in the old "Celtics style." The result of that plan was the 2008 NBA Championship—though this seemed to come as a shock to many of the pundits and so-called experts who evidently didn't know or had forgotten just what the "Celtics style" was about.

The style was created more than a half century ago by Arnold (Red) Auerbach when he took over a young franchise in the budding National Basketball Association. It was encapsulated 20 years later during the Bird era in the phrase "Celtics Pride."

Right above: *Rajon Rondo, here in the finals against the Lakers, really found his game in the 2008 playoffs.*

Right below: *One of the most dedicated players in Celtics history is John Havlicek. Now in the Hall of Fame, he played on eight NBA championship teams and remains the Celtics' all-time leader in games played and points scored.*

But that slogan became a bit tattered as the team's fortunes declined in the later eighties, throughout the nineties and into the new century.

Yet, without referring to it as such, "Celtics Pride" was a mantra that Rivers decided to follow in the 2007-08 championship season when he declared that his team would build its strength around defense. He understood, just as Auerbach did during eight of the 17 seasons when his Celtics became NBA champions, the truth of the old saw: Offense wins games, defense wins championships.

Rivers, like the Auerbachian disciples who preceded him as coach, also had a knack for convincing his players of the truth in another old adage: There is no "I" in Team. That lesson was a critical ingredient that Rivers used for the Celtics championship success in 2008. He convinced team captain Paul Pierce to become the chief proponent of this style in the locker room, where championships are won and lost because a team's approach to the game is first fashioned within its walls.

Watching Rivers' 2007-08 team was not very different than watching those from the other great Celtics eras. Only the names and faces had changed, but not the dedicated style of play. In short, basketball at the Garden was once again fun to watch.

It also helped to have an Auerbachian disciple in General Manager Danny Ainge, who orchestrated a strategy that remade a losing team into a world champion in just one season. Ainge learned his lessons well from being around Auerbach, who always sought players who could produce, played smart and always put team first, regardless of age or experience.

Ainge's education could be seen when the losing Celtics went from being the second youngest team in the NBA in 2007 to winning the championship as the fourth oldest team in the NBA in 2008. The group that Ainge assembled for Rivers was unselfish and did whatever it took to become champions. Most of that can be summed up in two words: Dedication, defense. These were the real heritage of Celtics basketball. And throughout the championship run of 2007-08, the Celtics greats of eras past looked on from the sidelines, reveling along with those on the floor in the return of Celtics Pride.

Could another Celtics dynasty bud in Boston with Pierce as its leader?

Undoubtedly Pierce will one day be inducted into the Hall of Fame, but for all the basketball feats that will make his entry possible, Boston will forever remember him for doing all that his coach asked of him to lead his team in returning the mantle of greatness to Celtics basketball.

Left: *Celtics rookie Tom Heinsohn lights coach Red Auerbach's traditional victory cigar after the team won its first Eastern Division title in 1957 en route to its first NBA championship.*

Below: *Paul Pierce and coach Doc Rivers celebrate after defeating the Lakers in Game 6 and clinching the 2008 NBA Championship.*

1. The Birth of the Green

The Boston Celtics have been the nation's most successful basketball team during most of the nearly half-century of their existence. It is, therefore, hard to believe that they were born into a hockey family whose head was Walter Brown and whose closest early siblings were men who, like Brown, ran ice hockey franchises in the National and American Hockey Leagues.

Brown was president of the Boston Bruins of the National Hockey League and head of the Boston Garden-Boston Arena Corporation. But as would always be true, Walter Brown was more than just a hockey buff. He was an avid sportsman who loved

ice hockey. Yet, after he became involved with the Celtics and Red Auerbach, he loved basketball with the same ardor.

While Brown was an avid sportsman, he was foremost a promoter, a man with acute instincts for finding ways to use his buildings as often as possible. Like his counterparts in other major cities in 1945, he sensed there was about to be a huge explosion in the American sports scene, and sought a way to exploit it. World War II had just ended, and the country was itching to wipe away the deprivations and gloom of four hard war years. At the same time, millions of servicemen were returning to civilian life, many of them athletes whose careers had been either interrupted or stopped in place by the war. They now created a glut that was spilling into both collegiate and professional arenas, waiting to be absorbed. Into the marketplace came two necessary elements for successful sports franchises: potential customers and potential performers. All they needed was a stage.

Professional hockey, in the form of the National Hockey League and American Hockey League, as well as some minor leagues, were the mainstays of arenas during the winter but only in a handful of cities from Chicago eastward. Pro basketball was the one area not fully exploited. It was mainly limited to weekend games played by the National Basketball League, which operated primarily in medium-sized cities in upstate New York and the Midwest; the American Basketball League, which played with declining interest along the eastern seaboard; and barnstorming teams like the Harlem Globetrotters.

It was under these circumstances in 1946 that Walter Brown, Ned Irish of Madison Square Garden, Al Sutphin of the Cleveland Arena, and eight other arena operators in Philadelphia, Providence, Toronto, Washington, Chicago, St. Louis, Detroit and Pittsburgh, formed the Basketball Association of America (BAA). In every city except Washington, there was already either a National or American Hockey League team, so the founders of this new basketball entity were, like Walter Brown, primarily hockey people who saw the possibility of keeping their buildings operating for another 30 nights each year.

Operating a building was one thing – and not all of those first 11 operators were successful in this new venture – but doing it on the level that Walter Brown did was something else. Had it not been for his tenacity and willingness to absorb annual losses during the team's early years, the Celtics easily could have gone the way of the Detroit Falcons, St. Louis Bombers, Pittsburgh Ironmen or the Toronto Huskies.

Ironically, during the team's first two seasons, college basketball, in the form of Holy Cross from Worcester, some 35 miles west of Boston, was the big draw at Boston Garden. The Crusaders, who won the

Above: *After Holy Cross defeated Oklahoma for the 1947 NCAA title at New York's Madison Square Garden, the Crusaders filled Boston Garden when they played basketball and helped to establish some feeling for the game in New England.*

Above: *The only two things the Boston Celtics ever had in common with the famed Original Celtics (shown above, in 1920) were the nickname and their great tradition of success. The Original Celtics were from New York.*

Right: *John "Honey" Russell, the Boston Celtics' first coach, was once a member of the Original Celtics. Here he is seen in 1927, when he was with the Chicago Bruins.*

NCAA championship in 1947 and made it back to the playoffs the following year, played before a capacity crowd of 13,909 fans at nearly every game. The Celtics, on the other hand, rarely drew more than 5,000 fans to a game. Brown lost more than

$350,000 during the team's first three seasons, but resisted the urgings of his associates to abandon the venture. Even after he hired Red Auerbach as head coach in 1950, and until he died in 1964, Brown never made much money with the Celtics – and that was after the team had won nine NBA titles in 10 years. But he never lost faith, though he often admitted there were times when it wore very thin.

Sometimes paychecks were late, and Brown once owed Auerbach $6,000 for an entire year before being able to pay him. No one complained, because the coach and his players knew that Brown had staked everything he owned on making the team successful, and they so appreciated his loyalty that they reciprocated in kind.

One of Brown's earliest decisions was what to name his new professional team. It is said that Brown and J. Howard McHugh, the new team's publicity director, discussed several names, such as the Unicorns, the Whirlwinds and the Olympics, but without much enthusiasm. Suddenly, Brown reached back into his sports memory and came up with the Celtics. "The name has great tradition in pro basketball because there was a great early team named the New York Celtics," he told McHugh. "And there are loads of Irishmen in Boston who would go for that name. We'll put them in green uniforms and call them the Boston Celtics." McHugh later said that he tried to talk Brown out of using the name because no team named after anything Irish had ever been successful in Boston. But his boss was unmoved, and so the Boston Celtics became one of the most famous names in sports history.

For his first head coach, Brown signed John (Honey) Russell, coach at Seton Hall, who had been a star with the Original Celtics and was still, at age 42, playing basketball with weekend leagues. There was no college draft that season so clubs had to scramble on their own to find players. One of those players was Kevin Charles Connors – later known to early television fans as Chuck Connors, "The Rifleman." Connors was the team's starting center, and also played baseball for the Brooklyn Dodgers long before his movie career as a western hero began in the early 1950s. The Celtics also had the NBA's only set of brothers – Connie and Johnny Simmons. Johnny Simmons also was a major league baseball player with the Washington Senators, while his brother later became a mainstay with the fine New York Knicks teams of the late 1940s and early 1950s.

The team also had to scramble to build its own playing floor, and because of wartime lumber shortages, carpenters scrounged around and could only come up with enough bits and pieces to build a parquet floor. Little did they know at the time that their scrap lumber product that cost $11,000 would become the team's hallmark for all time. During that first season (1946-47), it was transported back and forth between the Boston Garden and Boston Arena, where the Celtics played seven of their 30 home games because of scheduling conflicts. In fact, they played their first game at the Arena, which was located in the city's Back Bay area just around the corner from famed Symphony Hall, and lost to the Chicago Stags, 57-55.

The Celtics went on to lose their first five games, and 10 of their first 11, and finished the season with a 22-38 record, tied for last place in the Eastern Division with the Toronto Huskies – 27 games behind the division-leading Washington Capitols.

The first Celtics star appeared during the 1947-48 season. He was Ed Sadowski, a 30-year-old, cigar-smoking, 6-foot, 5-inch, 240-pound center who, along with Connors, had played for Russell at Seton Hall. He had started with the National Basketball League in 1940, and began the BAA's first

Above: *Jersey number 14 is among those retired by the Celtics after it was worn by Bob Cousy for 14 seasons. Eddie Ehlers (seen above, in 1948) was one of three others who also wore it.*

Left: *Alvin "Doggie" Julian was the Celtics' second head coach, for the 1948-49 and 1949-50 seasons.*

season as player-coach of the Toronto team. But he lasted just 12 games and was fired as coach, and then traded as a player to Cleveland. When Cleveland's franchise was disbanded after that first season, Sadowski was awarded to Boston and responded by averaging nearly 20 points a game and being named to the league's All-Star team.

That 1947-48 Celtics team also had some other interesting players. Their two top draft picks were Eddie Ehlers from Purdue and George Munroe from Dartmouth. Ehlers had received a $10,000 bonus from the New York Yankees, and also was selected by the Chicago Bears in the NFL draft. George Munroe had attended Harvard Law School and still is the only Rhodes Scholar in the Celtics' history. Another former Harvard player, Saul Mariaschin, finished second in Rookie of the Year voting. He also was a published songwriter, but was good enough on the court to finish among the league's top 10 playmakers. All of these team elements helped the Celtics make it to the playoffs for the first time, but despite playing all the games on their home court, they were eliminated in three games by the Stags.

Russell returned to Seton Hall after the 1948 season and Brown, looking at the success that Holy Cross had generated among a very small basketball following in Bos-

Right: *Ed Macauley leaps high into the air as he tries to intercept the ball from the Knicks' Vince Boryla in a 1950 game.*

Below: *Tony Lavelli came to the Celtics with a reputation for a great hook shot and a mean accordion. He provided the entertainment at halftime at many Celtics games, home and away.*

ton, hired the Crusaders' head coach, Alvin "Doggie" Julian. In January two of Julian's Holy Cross stars, George Kaftan and Dermott O'Connell, joined the Celtics and by season's end, with the two players adding some much needed talent, the Celtics' attendance had increased to nearly 5,000 per game.

Brown came up with another ploy the following season when he drafted Yale's Tony Lavelli, whose basketball talent was matched by his ability to play the accordion. Lavelli, a native of Somerville, Massachusetts, also had a deadly hook shot, and when he went to Yale, he was named to the

Helms All-America team in his freshman year. By his senior season, he was a consensus All-America, renowned for both the hook shot and the accordion.

Brown made him the Celtics' top draft pick for the 1949-50 season. Lavelli then negotiated a special contract by which he received $125 for a minimum of 25 halftime concerts around the National Basketball Association (the BAA and the NBL had merged after the 1949 season to form the NBA), including some during his own games. He was, noted some early observers from that time, the only player ever to have his performances covered in both the sports and entertainment sections of the next day's newspaper.

The high point came during his rookie season in a game against the defending champion Minneapolis Lakers at Boston Garden. He had scored just three points in the first half, and then after a halftime concert, he unloaded for 23 to help the Celtics

overcome a 15-point deficit and upset the mighty Lakers and their star, George Mikan. Though he was absolutely deadly with his hook shot – from as far away as 16 feet – the intense physical play in the pros continually threw off his timing, and he averaged just 6.9 points in two seasons with the team.

At the end of the 1949 season, the Celtics finished with their worst record ever, winning just 22 games and losing 46. Attendance was dismal, about 4,000 per game, and Brown fired Julian, who had angered him prior to the start of the season by cutting Ernie Calverley, the former Rhode Island star, after Brown had purchased the defunct Providence team just to secure his services.

That season, the Tri-Cities team management also got into a squabble with their head coach and he was soon looking for another job. That is when Brown and Red Auerbach found each other.

Left: *Tony Lavelli, a former All-America from Yale, was a local lad from nearby Somerville, whose cousin Dante Lavelli was a great end for pro football's Cleveland Browns.*

2. The Big Green Sees Red

It was April 27, 1950, and Arnold Jacob Auerbach, just hired as the Celtics' new head coach, was meeting Boston's sports media for the first time. They peppered him with questions about his players, always in the context of them as former New England collegians, and were particularly probing about why he was so lukewarm about Tony Lavelli, and why he had passed up the opportunity to draft Holy Cross star Bob Cousy. The parochialism quickly wore thin and Auerbach said to owner Walter Brown, for all of the media to hear, "Am I supposed to win or am I supposed to worry about the local yokels and please these guys?"

While the media were digesting that jolt, he continued: "I don't give a damn for sentiment or names. That goes for Cousy or anyone else. The only thing that counts with me is ability. I'm not interested in someone just because he happens to be a local yokel. That won't bring in more than a dozen extra fans on a regular basis. What will bring fans in is a winning team, and that's what I aim to have."

Boston, meet Red Auerbach.

Until that day, Boston knew very little about Auerbach, but they would soon find out that their new coach was a tough, determined, single-minded man who did things his way. For three seasons as head coach of the Washington Capitols, Auerbach had always turned out playoff teams, but had yet to produce a league champion. In 1949 he had taken over the Tri-Cities team that had gotten off to an 0-8 start, and he had his only losing season as a pro coach (28-29). Still, he did a great job considering that his team had no pre-season training under his scrutiny but still made the playoffs.

That achievement was indicative of the way Auerbach coached any team, never intimidated or influenced by a player's age or experience, but always insisting on solid

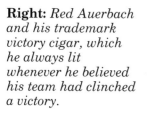

Right: *Red Auerbach and his trademark victory cigar, which he always lit whenever he believed his team had clinched a victory.*

fundamentals and an attack style of basketball geared to one thing: success. And he achieved it in epic proportions; he won NBA championships in nine of his 16 years as the team's head coach. What makes the record so distinctive – and probably unreachable for all time – was that eight of those championships were consecutive (and the nine came within a 10-season span). This success came with no frills or great resources. He knew exactly what it took to win, and he was single-minded and unyielding in pursuing that goal. His team's success, even when it had come so many years in succession that any coach and his players could have become overconfident, was always exciting. Under Auerbach's hard-driving tutelage, the Celtics always seemed to be a team on a mission, not one defending a championship.

The consistent success of his team was as much a tribute to Auerbach as to the great players who performed under his direction. He was the team's only coach and chief scout. The only trappings of success he indulged in were the world championship banners that he gleefully hoisted to the ceiling of Boston Garden every year. To Auerbach, those banners represented what he and the Celtics were all about.

During his coaching reign, and for many years thereafter, the team's office was located at the top of a stairway that led to the playing court of Boston Garden. During many of those early years, the Celtics' office harbored just two full-time employees: J. Howard McHugh, the publicity director, and a secretary. Auerbach spent only the basketball season in Boston, living in a sparsely furnished room at a hotel in the Back Bay section. The rest of the time he spent on the road with his team or scouting, or at his home in Washington, D.C. That regimen never changed.

He dressed his teams simply, all green (away) or all white (home), with no frills after he discarded the shamrock that decorated the shorts. He deliberately chose black sneakers because they were easier to keep clean than white ones, and they soon became one of the team's hallmarks. He was never bashful about winning and about letting people know who deserved the credit. That is one reason why he always lit his cigar when he believed his team had a victory in hand, though the game was still ongoing. Forget the No Smoking signs – the cigar sent a message that the game was over and the coach was enjoying the fruits of his labor.

No one who played for Auerbach ever doubted for a minute that he was the boss. Neither did anyone who ever played against his teams, or officiated in those games. Like many of sport's great coaches, he ardently resented the slightest impediment to his team's success. He was intolerant of mental errors, lack of effort and the inability to produce under the pressure of a game. He was a stickler for fundamentals,

Below left: *There never was a more fiery competitor than Red Auerbach. He coached the Celtics for 16 seasons, winning 795 games and nine NBA titles.*

Below: *Bob Cousy was a member of the NCAA championship team at Holy Cross as a freshman in 1947.*

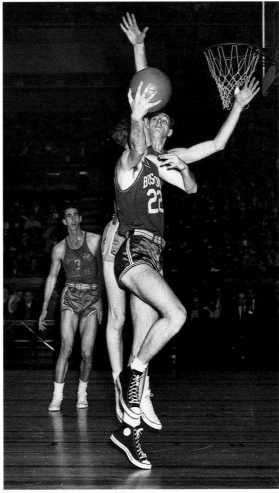

and drilled his teams to produce defense, constant movement on offense and hard work under the boards to produce rebounds at both ends of the court.

Although Auerbach's teams were not always the most talented from end-to-end, for his final 10 seasons as head coach of the Celtics, he had the game's greatest player at that time, center Bill Russell. The rest of Auerbach's players were drilled to precision in a system that was relatively simple. "We only had seven plays," Auerbach once recalled, "and even our opponents knew them. But they couldn't stop them because we executed them so precisely."

And that is the way the Celtics always played under Auerbach, beginning with the very first season in 1950, when he brought them to a playoff with their first winning record. Walter Brown had begun to lay the groundwork for success even before Auerbach arrived when, with the first pick of the draft he selected 6-foot, 11-inch center Charley Share from Bowling Green College in Ohio, stunning New Englanders by passing up Cousy. He then stunned the entire NBA by selecting forward Chuck Cooper of Duquesne – the first black player ever selected by the league. He then cancelled his acquisition of Share by selecting center Ed Macauley in a dispersal draft from the defunct St. Louis Bombers.

As a rookie, Macauley had been called the league's second-best center, behind the Lakers' George Mikan. In his first season in Boston, he became the first Celtics player ever to average 20 points a game, and was a solid scorer during his six seasons with the team. But he was never physically strong enough to be the dominant rebounder that Auerbach needed to make his style of play successful. While he later was traded as part of another amazing deal that brought Bill Russell to Boston, his services were always appreciated by Auerbach. His jersey number, 22, hangs above the Garden's floor with banners from the great Celtics teams, though he was never a part of their successes.

Chuck Cooper's acquisition in the second round of the 1950 draft was pro basketball's equivalent of Jackie Robinson being signed just four years earlier by the Brooklyn Dodgers because, like Robinson, he was a pioneer for his race in the NBA. The pressure at that time to exclude blacks came not from any established prejudice by fans or owners, but fear of displeasure from the powerful Harlem Globetrotters organization, which was the world's most famous touring basketball team, and was composed entirely of the best black players who could be found. The league needed the Globetrotters to help draw fans into their buildings

Opposite: *Chuck Cooper (dark uniform, at left), battles the Knicks for a rebound during a 1950 game.*

Above left: *Cooper, who had played for Duquesne, was drafted by the Celtics in 1950 and was the first black player in NBA history.*

Above: *Easy Ed Macauley (22) was the Celtics' first great scorer. His jersey was retired by Red Auerbach, though he never played on a Celtics championship team.*

Above: *Chuck Cooper (with ball) beats the Knicks' George Kaftan for a rebound. Rookies Cooper and Bob Cousy (14) led the Celtics to the playoffs in 1950.*

in those years as the opening part of a doubleheader, so the owners were very careful not to do anything from a business sense that would jeopardize those guaranteed paydays.

Of course, The Globetrotters reacted against Brown and told him they never again would play in the Boston Garden. "That's fine with me," was Brown's response, "because as far as I'm concerned, you are no longer welcome in the Boston Garden."

That was only one battle fought and won. Cooper had many, none of which was different than those being fought by other black players who were integrating professional sports teams at that time. In some cities, he had to stay in a separate hotel than his teammates. In Washington and St. Louis, he stayed in the same hotel with the team, but was forbidden from eating in the hotel's dining room. So Auerbach told him to call room service for his meals. Often, his teammates ate with him in his room, and at all times, he had the complete support of everyone in the organization.

The biggest move toward success came later in the fall of 1950 when Chicago's

franchise folded and there was another dispersal draft for the benefit of Boston, New York and Philadelphia, the three worst teams from the previous season. The three most coveted players from that team were Max Zaslofsky, Andy Phillip and Bob Cousy, who had been traded by Auerbach's old Tri-Cities team to the Stags. NBA president Maurice Podoloff placed the names of the three players into a hat and, disdaining the first pick because he had had it in an earlier draft, Brown went last and got Cousy for $8,500 – and with him a new dimension to the game.

Auerbach had always believed that the 6-foot, 1-inch Cousy was a detriment because of his size, and he told him from the outset, "You're a little man playing in a big man's game, and you have two strikes on you for that reason." It wasn't until Cousy had helped Boston to its first NBA title in 1957 that Auerbach agreed that he did indeed have the best ballhandler in the game's history, a player who was given such nicknames as "Houdini of the Hardwood," and "The Mobile Magician."

His famed behind-the-back passes became a trademark of sorts, and every young basketball player in the 1950s spent hours trying to emulate him. But there was only one Cousy, a man who directed needle-eye passes from any part of the court, fired up shots from 25 or 30 feet and was as close to a genius in directing a game as any who ever played. Put a ball in his hands, and there was no telling what he would do with it – dribble it between his legs, fire it behind his back, or take off toward the basket and drop it for a trailing player who swooped in for a shot. By the end of his third NBA season Cousy did things with a basketball that Auerbach said had never been envisioned, let alone ever seen.

He was a master dribbler and once dribbled the ball through and around a New York Knicks team for the final 23 seconds of a game to secure a one-point victory. But one of his most memorable games was a four-overtime playoff victory over Syracuse in 1953; he played 66 of the game's 68 minutes and scored 50 points, demonstrating that despite his alleged lack of size, he was a remarkably durable player (he once held the NBA record for most minutes played). In that game, two of his 30 free throws (in 32 attempts) tied the game with two seconds to play in regulation time. He scored six of his team's eight points in the first overtime, including a tie-making foul with one second to play, got two of his team's four points in the final seconds of the second overtime to force another tie, and in an incredible display of clutch play, scored five points in the final 13 seconds of the third overtime to force a third tie. Three came on a three-point play with five seconds to play, and his other two after he intercepted the inbounds pass and heaved up a shot from 30 feet just as the buzzer sounded. And in the final overtime period, he got nine of the Celtics' 12 points as Boston won, 111-105.

There were many times, such as in that game, when Cousy showed he was a prolific scorer. His scoring prowess was always secondary, however, because his other talents were so great, and because of Auer-

bach's insistence that his team spread its offense among all players and give equal concentration on defense.

While his impact as a rookie was not close to what it became during the Celtics' dynasty seasons, Cousy nonetheless formed a near triumvirate with Macauley and Cooper that had a direct hand in helping Boston to a 39-30 record in 1950-51. After battling Philadelphia for the Eastern Division title during the entire season, the team fell just short, and then lost in the first round of the playoffs.

Below: *Bob Cousy, who was bypassed by the Celtics in the 1950 draft because of his size, was acquired later that year when his original team folded. He became one of the greatest guards in NBA history.*

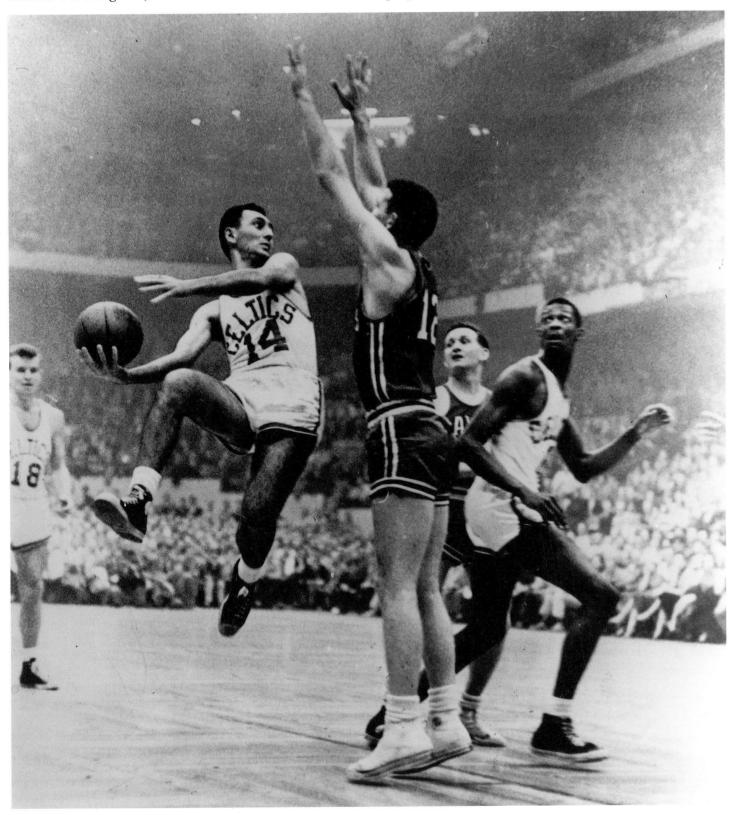

Above: *Cousy led the Celtics' fast break offense with his superb ball handling and passing, and was renowned for his ability to pass the ball behind his back.*

Right: *Bill Sharman (21) formed a great guard tandem with Cousy during the early part of the Celtics' dynasty.*

decided to try out his other love, and went to winter baseball before reporting to the Dodgers' farm team at St. Paul. He reported to the Dodgers in early September with the promise of some action. But Brooklyn soon blew a 13-and-a-half game lead, and Sharman never got into the game.

The Pistons, wary of his baseball ambitions, gladly traded his rights to the Celtics, and Auerbach then convinced him to forego the diamond for the parquet. Auerbach teamed him with Cousy in the season's first game in 1951, and they stayed as basketball's number one back-court tandem until Sharman finally retired in 1961. He didn't have Cousy's flair for ballhandling, but he was one of the greatest shooters in Celtics history, particularly with a one-handed jump shot, and from the foul line where he compiled an NBA record 88.3 percent accuracy mark. Cousy once described him as "a perpetual motion man" because he never stopped moving, with or without the ball, and he was an ideal target for Cousy's ball-handling wizardry.

But the enduring legacy of the new-look Celtics during the first half of the 1950s was the way they personified Auerbach's exciting style of basketball, gradually transforming into a powerhouse to delight the many avid Boston fans.

The next step after the acquisitions of Cousy, Macauley and Cooper occurred in 1951 when Bill Sharman, who had been a star basketball player at the University of Southern California (but a more promising pro baseball player), joined the team. Like other moves that he used to build his great teams, Auerbach's intricate dealing for Sharman included many components, including the acquisition of burly forward Bob Brannum. The deal came via a circuitous route that centered around Auerbach's trading Share's rights to the Fort Wayne Pistons for Bob Harris, $10,000 in cash and a player to be named later. Auerbach used the $10,000 to purchase Brannum, who became the first of his "enforcers." The role of Auerbach's enforcers was to guard the opposition's top-scoring forward – "soften him up" was often a more apt description – and also to act as "policeman" if opponents were mauling any of the Celtics.

The "player to be named later" became Sharman, who had broken all of Hank Luisetti's Pacific Coast Conference scoring records and had started the 1950 NBA season with the Washington Capitols. That team folded in mid-season and Sharman was picked up by the Pistons, but he

Left: *Though a slick ball handler and playmaker, Cousy never was afraid to take the ball into the teeth of a defense, as he does here against the Knicks' Harry Gallatin (11), Ernie Vandeweghe and Sweetwater Clifton during a 1952 game.*

3. Russell

While the Celtics of the early 1950s were an entertaining and energetic team that featured Red Auerbach's fast-break style of basketball, they also were a very frustrated team. The Celts had made the playoffs with winning records during his first six seasons, but they could not win an NBA championship.

Consider their record during these years: In 1950 Boston finished second in the Eastern Division, but didn't win a playoff against the Knicks. In 1951 they finished second again, but once more were eliminated in the first round of the playoffs. In 1952 they had their third straight second-place finish, but lost to New York in the first round of the playoffs after Bill Sharman was sidelined with the measles. In 1953 they finished third, yet made it to the divisional finals before losing to Syracuse. In 1954 they finished second and missed the final again when they were eliminated in a round robin playoff. In 1955 they were third and again made the division finals before

being eliminated by the Nats in four games. In 1956 they were second for a fifth time, but lost to Syracuse in the first round of the playoffs.

The reason was apparent: the team needed someone to dominate the backboards. Ed Macauley was a fine scorer at center but he was not strong enough to bang the boards night after night. By the end of a season, he was beaten up and ineffective in the playoffs. In 1954 the NBA also had instituted the 24-second clock, so teams had many more shots and Macauley could not take the additional pounding.

Auerbach sought a bigger, stronger center, but not necessarily one who could match Macauley's scoring, because the team had plenty of firepower. It finally was Macauley's own desire to return to his native St. Louis, where his son was critically ill, that set into motion the one great trade that made the Celtics a dynasty.

Bill Russell came to Boston.

Russell was an All-America center at the University of San Francisco, who had helped the Dons to two consecutive national championships and a 56-game unbeaten streak. The Rochester Royals, last in the NBA in 1956, had first draft rights to him, but Russell snuffed out that deal by demanding a salary of $25,000. In the meantime, Auerbach had received glowing

reports on him as a player and team performer, and worked out a deal with Ben Kerner, owner of the St. Louis Hawks (and his old boss at Tri-Cities with whom he still feuded) to trade Macauley and rookie guard Cliff Hagan for Russell's draft rights. Auerbach then got the NBA owners to waive the rule against trading a number one draft choice by convincing them that this trade would benefit both teams. They agreed — and there was a new name in Boston's sports lexicon: Russell.

Many in the NBA at that time considered Russell a one-dimensional college player who excelled on defense but was not much of a scorer. The defensive aspect of the game was not appreciated as much then as it is now — except by Auerbach. He had enough offense but he wanted someone who could control the backboards and dictate the pace of the game by triggering his fast-break offense with great rebounding skill from some much-needed defense.

Russell, who had originally wanted to play for the Minneapolis Lakers, was delighted when Boston drafted him and signed a $22,500 contract, from which $6,000 originally was deducted because he missed the first two months of the season while playing for the nation's 1956 Olympic gold medal basketball team in Australia. Walter Brown later restored

Above: *Chuck Cooper (11) shoots over the Syracuse Nats during a 1953 game. He and Macauley helped the Celtics to the NBA playoffs during their four seasons together.*

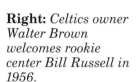
Right: *Celtics owner Walter Brown welcomes rookie center Bill Russell in 1956.*

Below: *Russell's great rebounding and defensive skills revolutionized the pro game and were the key ingredients to the team's 11 NBA championships during his 13 seasons.*

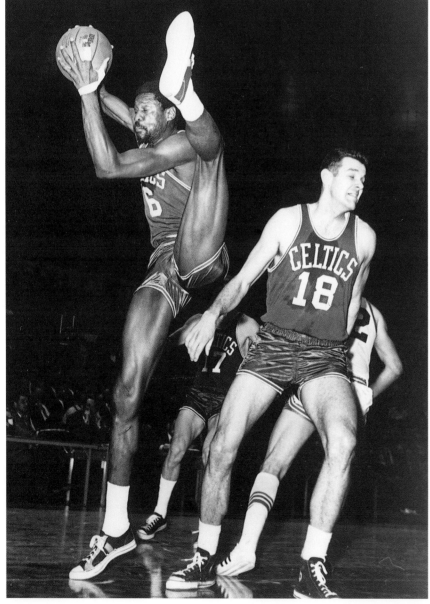

that amount, telling him, "Why should I penalize you when you were doing so much for our country?"

Russell – and that was how he was always referred to by teammate and foe – did just as much for the Celtics for the next 13 seasons. Most of all, he changed the way in which the game was played. He was a marvelous 6-foot, 10-inch athlete, whose great arm spread and leaping ability made him more like 7-foot-2. With his extraordinary physical grace he single-handedly made rebounding and shot-blocking a new art form in professional basketball. Other centers blocked shots, but Russell had the skill to direct the ball into a teammate's hands rather than just to swat it out of bounds. Opponents became reluctant to test that ability, or to penetrate too close to the basket lest they find the ball being stuffed back into their faces. The Celtics set up their defense to funnel everything into the middle, where Russell was an unflinching keeper of the basket, forcing teams to find new ways to run their offense.

"He made every center in the league a better player whenever they played against him," said Wayne Embry, a great center for the Cincinnati Royals. "You psyched yourself up to play him and you knew you had to be at your very best, if not better, just to stay with him. He even made me develop an outside shot because my inside game simply didn't work against him.

"Russell was very serious on the court but he always respected anyone with ability, and if you beat him on a shot, he'd sometimes say, 'You got me that time.' But then he'd go out and get you 10 more times.

"One of the happiest days of my life came when I joined him as a teammate. He brought out the best in everyone and motivated them by his action. I once saw him block a shot after being 10 yards behind the guy, and I found myself looking for someone I could do the same thing to."

Russell was an absolutely unselfish player, and a fierce competitor who sometimes worked himself into such a state before a game that he would be sick. "Whenever we heard Russell in the bathroom throwing up, we knew we were in for a good night," Auerbach once said. "If we didn't hear anything, we knew there could be trouble."

When he finally finished his playing career in 1969, he was the NBA's all-time rebounder with 21,620 (he now ranks third behind Kareem Abdul-Jabbar and Wilt Chamberlain, each of whom played many more seasons) and scored 14,522 points, a 15.1 per game average. That was perfect in the Celtics' style because Auerbach never sought top-heavy scorers, just five or six

guys who would hit double figures in every game and play the roles he designed for them.

He got a couple more of those players when Tom Heinsohn and Frank Ramsey joined the Celtics, with Russell, in 1957. Heinsohn was a star center at Holy Cross, but Auerbach wanted him to play forward on his team. After getting his agreement to join the Celtics for a $9,000 salary, Auerbach made him a territorial pick, meaning no other team could draft him. Heinsohn was well worth the price, and was an ideal player for Auerbach's team. He filled a big void caused by Macauley's departure because he supplied the lost scoring, added more rebounding, and enabled Russell to concentrate on defense. He earned the nickname "Tommy Gun" because he was never bashful taking shots. He had a great line drive shot that he had developed as a kid in New Jersey because the hall in which he played had such a low ceiling that he had to use a low trajectory.

Heinsohn also was Auerbach's kind of player because he never backed down from

Above: *Bill Russell (6) wasn't famous for his offense, but he averaged a respectable 15 points per game.*

Left: *Red Auerbach and Tom Heinsohn celebrate the Celtics' first NBA title, 125-123 in double overtime over St. Louis, in 1957.*

anyone. He worked hard, he was resilient and he had the kind of personality that enabled Auerbach to make him his "whipping boy" without it ever affecting his play. Auerbach used this cleverly to get his message to other players: "If Auerbach can do that to a player of Heinsohn's stature, what will he do to me?"

"Red Auerbach could get more out of people with less effort than any man I've ever known in my life," Heinsohn said. "That was his secret as a coach. He knew what made every guy tick, and he knew that some of the big guys had sensitive egos that didn't like it if Red started to get on them verbally.

"So when he wanted to get on someone to stir things in the dressing room, he got on me. He knew I could take it. I was his whipping boy. I understood what he was doing so I could handle it."

One night Heinsohn had a great first half, scoring more than 20 points, grabbed a dozen rebounds and a half dozen assists. Yet at halftime Auerbach started to chew him out, and he took it for a while before finally asking him, "Hey Red, what the hell have I done wrong tonight?"

Auerbach looked at him for a moment and then, with a straight face, said, "You warmed up lousy."

The Celtics got one other bonus late in the 1957 season when Frank Ramsey returned from army duty and took the role of "sixth man." He had played during the 1954 season before going into the military, and when he rejoined the team Auerbach had plenty of talent, so he came up with a scheme to get the best non-starter who was both a good shooter and an up-tempo player into the game. The rationale was that Ramsey – and every "sixth man" thereafter – would face a player not as fresh and unable to cope with someone bursting with offensive energy. Auerbach repeated the sequence often in a game, forcing the opposing coach either to lift the tired player for someone fresh, but not as talented as the Celtics' sixth man, or force his tired player to cope. That often resulted in cheap fouls or the player giving away too much. Either way, Auerbach got the edge.

Ramsey was the perfect example of an Auerbach role player because not starting didn't bother him. In fact, he preferred to see how the game's tempo was evolving before he played, and then he adjusted his own tempo accordingly. At times when he had to start, he admitted that he simply wasn't as comfortable or as effective.

Auerbach thus had finally put together the contending team he wanted during the 1950s, with Russell at center, Heinsohn and Jim Loscutoff as forwards, Bob Cousy and Sharman as guards, and the talented Ramsey coming off the bench to keep things moving. He backed them up with veteran Arnie Risen, who had played center until Russell arrived and then unselfishly tutored the rookie in the ways of the position, Andy Phillip, Jack Nichols, Lou Tsioropoulos and Dick Hemric.

But embodying the Celtic spirit and unifying the team was one man: Russell.

Opposite: *Tom Heinsohn (15) was nicknamed "Tommy Gun" for his prolific offense. Here, he overwhelms the Lakers' Rudy La Russo in 1959.*

Below: *The Celtics' first world championship team in 1957. From left, first row: Lou Tsioropoulos, Andy Phillip, Frank Ramsey, coach Red Auerbach, Bob Cousy, Bill Sharman, Jim Loscutoff. Second row: President Walter Brown, Dick Hemric, Jack Nichols, Bill Russell, Arnie Risen, Tom Heinsohn, trainer Harvey Cohn, and VP Lou Pieri.*

4. The Dynasty Begins

Below: *Coach Red Auerbach chats with Bill Russell and his wife Rose in 1956. Auerbach still calls Russell the greatest player in NBA history.*

The Bill Russell era didn't really begin until one-third of the 1957 season was over, when Russell finally reported after finishing his Olympic Games commitment and getting married. But the season had gotten off to a good start without him because the Celtics were in first place in the Eastern Division with a 16-8 record. Coach Red Auerbach had worked around the center problem by using veterans Arnie Risen and Jack Nichols, and on occasion, Tom Heinsohn.

Once Russell arrived, his inexperience didn't seem to slow down the march because he easily fit into the Celtics' system and his defense was startling. Thus, the Celtics won their first division title – helped by an eight-game winning streak in January after Frank Ramsey returned from his army hitch – and finished with a 44-28 record, the best in the NBA.

There was no magic involved in their success, not with a front line of Russell, Heinsohn and Jim Loscutoff; and with Bob Cousy and Bill Sharman in the back court; and Ramsey coming off the bench as sixth man. The only fear in Auerbach's mind was his team not breaking the playoff jinx that had haunted it for the previous six seasons. Boston put that to rest by sweeping the Syracuse Nats. They then faced the St. Louis Hawks, now led by former Celtics Charley Share, Ed Macauley and Cliff Hagan, and featuring one of the NBA's

Left: *Jack Nichols (16) snags the ball from the hands of the Knicks' Willie Naulls in 1958. Naulls would join the Celtics in 1964.*

Below: *Tom Heinsohn was a fierce inside player as both a scorer, here against St. Louis in the 1957 NBA finals, and as a rebounder. He scored 12,194 points and had 5,749 rebounds during his career.*

greatest players, forward Bob Pettit.

The teams traded victories, and after Hagan had tipped in the winning basket at the buzzer in game six in St. Louis, the title finally came down to what may well be the most memorable seventh game the Celtics ever played for an NBA title. Russell and Heinsohn, always clutch playoff players, were the deciding factors for Boston as Cousy and Sharman came up ice cold in this game, making only five of 40 shots. Heinsohn picked up the slack with 37 points and 23 rebounds while Russell added 32 rebounds and 19 points. One of the game's most dramatic plays occurred in the final minute when the Hawks' Jack Coleman tried to drive for a basket that would have given St. Louis a three-point lead, but Russell blocked his shot, sprinted to the other end of the court and scored a basket that gave Boston a one-point lead.

But Cousy, always a good foul shooter and usually impervious to pressure, lost a chance to put the game away when he missed one of two foul shots with 13 seconds to play, and Boston led by two points. With six seconds to play, Sharman, in the same emotional morass as Cousy, missed his favorite jump shot and the chance to win the game in regulation time. Pettit then made two foul shots with three seconds left to tie the score at 113-113, and Sharman missed a 25-footer at the end of the regulation that again could have won the game.

Heinsohn nailed three shots in the

Right: *Tom Heinsohn, who had scored 37 points and grabbed 23 rebounds before fouling out with two minutes to play in the second overtime of the 1957 title game against St. Louis, can't bear to watch the final seconds as Boston won 125-123 for their first world championship.*

second overtime, including his 20-foot jumper that put Boston ahead 121-120, before fouling out with two minutes to play. St. Louis tied the score but Ramsey's field goal and foul moved Boston ahead, 124-121, before the Hawks cut the advantage to 124-123 with 27 seconds to play. Player-coach Alex Hannum turned over the ball trying to get it in to Pettit with eight seconds to play, and Loscutoff seemingly nailed down the win with a foul shot for a 125-123 lead with one second left.

But no lead was safe in this game; Hannum, putting the ball into play, heaved it off the Celtics' backboard and it bounced right into Pettit's hands. He rushed a shot from the foul lane that just skidded off the basket.

It was difficult to say whether the Celtics' chief emotions were relief or joy. Russell and Loscutoff picked up Auerbach, who was still ashen from Pettit's near miss, and carried him off the court. Heinsohn was also carried aloft, while Cousy and Sharman, the frustration of past seasons finally lifted, whooped up a storm. What none of those principals, nor the thousands of Celtics fans at the Garden, realized was that this was just the beginning of the greatest dynasty run in sports history, and that it wouldn't always – although occasionally it would – be this dramatic.

That quickly became a fact the following season when, tied 1-1 with the Hawks in the NBA finals, Russell suffered a chipped bone fracture of his left ankle, and was forced to sit and watch the Celtics lose in six games. "Russell's absence wasn't the reason we lost," a gracious Auerbach said. "We were beaten by a great team and they deserved to win."

He was correct, though it will always be a moot point whether a healthy Russell, surrounded by the Celtics' strong supporting cast, would have made it two titles in a row. Boston had added only one rookie that season, 24-year-old Sam Jones from little North Carolina College, whose greatest days still lay ahead. He was gun shy as a shooter during his early seasons, but would finish his career in 1969 as the team's second all-time scorer with over 18,000 points. With Cousy and Sharman in the back court during his early seasons, there weren't always a lot of opportunities. But once they retired, Jones became the team's principal back court scorer, probably the most natural shooter the team had until Larry Bird. His shooting seemed almost effortless when he lofted a jump shot from his "sweet spot" on the left side of the court, about 15 feet from the basket, always banking it off the backboard with almost monotonous ease. He also was one of the great

clutch shooters in Celtics history, and like all great clutch players he always wanted the ball when a key shot was needed late in the game – be it a regular-season game or the seventh game of the NBA finals.

The Celtics got another Jones the following year when K. C. Jones, Russell's teammate on the University of San Francisco NCAA champion team and U.S. Olympic team, discarded a potentially bright career as a defensive back with the Los Angeles Rams. After graduation from USF, K. C., who had been drafted by the Celtics, had served two years in the army, where he also played football and basketball. One of his football teammates was John Morrow, a center for the Rams, and he told his team that Jones was a solid prospect. The Rams' general manager was Pete Rozelle, who had been the Dons' publicity man during K.C.'s early college years, and who knew him well enough himself to sign him as a free agent, though he had only high school and service ball experience. Still, he was talented enough to start the team's first three exhibition games as a defensive back, before injuring his leg. Jones balked at Coach Sid Gillman's insistence that he play despite the injury, and he decided to answer Auerbach's pleas to play for the Celtics. And though it had been three years since he had played college ball, he made the Celtics

Above: *One of the Celtics' two "Jones Boys" – Sam – drives for a basket against the Royals' Oscar Robertson.*

Left: *K.C. Jones – the other Jones Boy – was the Celtics' best defensive guard during his 10 seasons, and drew the opposition's best shooting guard.*

because, as Auerbach said, "Something good always seemed to happen whenever he got into the game."

"When Red pointed his finger at me to go into the ball game, I knew he wanted ferocious defense on the other team's toughest guard, as well as sharp, crisp passes and all the hustle I had," Jones later wrote. "I gave

Above: *The Celtics and Lakers always were fierce NBA title foes. Here, Bob Cousy drives between Jerry West and Elgin Baylor in a playoff game.*

Right: *Bill Sharman, who later became a successful Lakers' head coach, plants a kiss on Bob Cousy's cheek after the Celtics defeated the Lakers in the 1959 finals.*

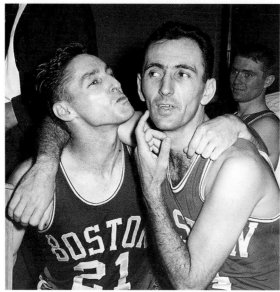

the team all I had, and I made sure I was always ready."

K. C. Jones was the final peg in putting together the greatest Celtics team in history. The team's dynasty would continue, with some changes, a domination of the NBA that lasted through all but one year of the 1960s. But no Celtics teams were ever as dominant as those from 1957-58 through 1962-63, which won 286 of 386 regular-season games, and 40 of 61 playoff games. They won five consecutive division titles by an average of 11 games.

In 1959, the Celtics were motivated by a determination to regain their lost NBA championship, and they did it by winning 52 of their 72 games. Boston had averaged a record 116.4 points per game, including a record-setting 173-129 victory over the Minneapolis Lakers. So stunning was the immensity of that victory that NBA commissioner Maurice Podoloff launched an investigation to see if the game was on the up-and-up, a move that infuriated Auerbach because it called into question not only his integrity and that of his team, but of the sport itself.

Loscutoff, who had played only five games the previous season, was healthy, and was joined by Gene Conley, who had spent five seasons playing major league baseball, where he had helped the Milwaukee Braves to a World Series title in 1957. There never were two tougher players on one team, and they gave the Celtics plenty of intimidation muscle.

The Celtics needed it against the Syracuse Nats that year, who took Boston to seven games in the semifinals. The Celtics fell behind by 16 points in the second quarter of the seventh game; were up by eight midway through the final quarter; fell back by three later in the quarter; and then put together a five-point burst by Cousy and Russell to wrest the lead for good. Russell fouled out with two minutes to play and Conley came on for some fine pivot play, nailing three crucial rebounds during those final minutes and getting Auerbach's accolade as the "man who saved the playoffs for us," as Boston won 130-125.

It was easy after that because the Celtics, who had beaten the Lakers 22 straight times, were at their best in their four-game sweep. The two teams battled each other for the NBA championship six more times during the Russell era, and the Celtics won every series.

However, the following season, the Celtics faced another formidable force when Wilt Chamberlain joined the Philadelphia Warriors as a rookie, and immediately became Russell's foremost personal rival. Chamberlain was a schoolboy legend in Philadelphia and had helped the University of Kansas to the NCAA finals in 1957. He left the Jayhawks to play with the Harlem Globetrotters before the Warriors made him a territorial draft pick.

Chamberlain was always listed at 7-feet, 1-inch tall, but those who played against him swore he was at least two or three inches taller. He packed a solid 270 pounds on that huge frame and every ounce of it seemed to be muscle. The first time Russell and Chamberlain faced each other occurred early in the 1959-60 season when the 5-0 Warriors came to Boston to face the 3-0 Celtics. As happened in all of their future meetings, Boston Garden was jammed, and this time the Boston fans got their money's worth as Russell out-rebounded his taller foe, 35-28, and brought down the house when he even blocked one of Chamberlain's shots. Wilt outscored Russell 30-22, but the Warriors lost, 115-105.

"I've played against centers that big, but never against any as big and as good," Russell said later. "He's the best rookie I've ever seen."

Chamberlain had stunned Russell in that game when both players grabbed a loose ball and Wilt lifted him off the floor before the referee called for a jump ball.

"The thought flashed through my mind that I'm going to look awfully silly if he stuffs the ball and me through the basket," he said later, cackling his distinctive laugh. But from that time on, Russell never said anything to stir up his formidable rival, and he always played down any advantages that he and his teams enjoyed over Chamberlain's teams.

Russell had a decided edge in his duels against Chamberlain because they were always battles of minds as much as physical skills, and no player in the NBA during those years was tougher mentally than Bill Russell. Had Chamberlain matched Rus-

Above: *Bill Russell (6) vs. Wilt Chamberlain (13) became the greatest man-on-man confrontation in NBA history.*

Left: *Bill Russell battles the St. Louis Hawks in the Celtics' title-clinching victory at Boston Garden in 1960.*

Above: *Bob Cousy was a member of six Celtics NBA championship teams. Here, Boston Garden fans give him a ride off the court after Boston defeated St. Louis for the 1960 NBA title.*

sell's determination, he would have eclipsed the Celtics' center. Scoring points was more important to Chamberlain than the other parts of the game, but it was just the opposite for Russell, who reveled in team play. During the 10 seasons they faced each other, Russell's teams won 58 and lost 41 games against Chamberlain's, and only twice in that time did Wilt hold a season advantage. One other time, in 1967, the teams split. In the playoffs Russell's Celtics lost only once in seven series, but the success of their duels is best measured by Russell's commanding 9-1 edge in NBA championships over Chamberlain's teams in Philadelphia, San Francisco and Los Angeles.

Chamberlain was a formidable obstacle in the 1960 Eastern Division playoffs after the Celtics had blitzed the division. Boston was on a roll after winning 30 of its first 34 games en route to a fourth straight title, during which they hit an all-time NBA best of 124.5 points per game. Cousy had one of his greatest seasons with a career-high 9.4 assists per game, and he became the first player in NBA history to accumulate 5,000 assists. Russell had a 51-rebound game against Syracuse, and then helped the Celtics eliminate Chamberlain and the Warriors in six games of the conference finals. Wilt hurt his own cause – and himself – when he tried to punch out Heinsohn. The Celtic wisely ducked and Wilt broke his hand when it struck the back of teammate Tom Gola's head. The St. Louis Hawks still were in their prime, and they took Boston to seven games before Russell's 35 rebounds and 22 points led the Celtics to a 122-103 title game victory.

In 1960-61, the Celtics won the division title by 11 games, and then eliminated both Syracuse and the Hawks in five games in the playoffs. The Syracuse series was marred by a 10-minute brawl involving Celtics players and the fans, and requiring the services of Syracuse police and ushers.

Auerbach called the 1960-61 team "the best ever assembled" after it had defeated St. Louis in a title-clinching 121-112 victory, with Russell contributing 38 rebounds and 30 points. While such praise often is spoken in the euphoria of victory, Auerbach was probably correct; no Boston team ever won a title in such leisurely fashion. That title also marked the first "changing of the guard" because Bill Sharman, who was 34, retired after the playoffs. Auerbach had been giving Sam Jones more experience, and the following season Jones became a starter.

Auerbach had already shored up the forward position with number one draft pick Tom "Satch" Sanders from New York University. Like Heinsohn, he had been a center in college but was moved to forward by Auerbach, where his instincts and reflexes made him one of the best defensive forwards in the team's history. For years he was assigned the opposition's top scorer – Elgin Baylor, Bob Pettit, Chet Walker, it didn't matter – and he did the job.

Of course, Satch also became a bit of a legend. He and K. C. Jones used to wager which of them could do the best defensive job on the player they were guarding – and when they played the Lakers that often meant Jones worked on Jerry West while Sanders took Baylor. The intensity of their work was awesome as the lean and lanky Sanders used arms, legs, hands – every part of his body that he felt would do the job.

Sanders also kept the team loose with his low-key sense of humor. When the team was staying in Washington during the 1962 season, they received an informal invita-

Above: *Tom (Satch) Sanders (16) was a fine all-around forward who also got the job of defending the opposition's top scorer.*

Left: *The Celtics visited their number one fan – President John F. Kennedy (center) – at the Oval Office in the White House during the 1962 season.*

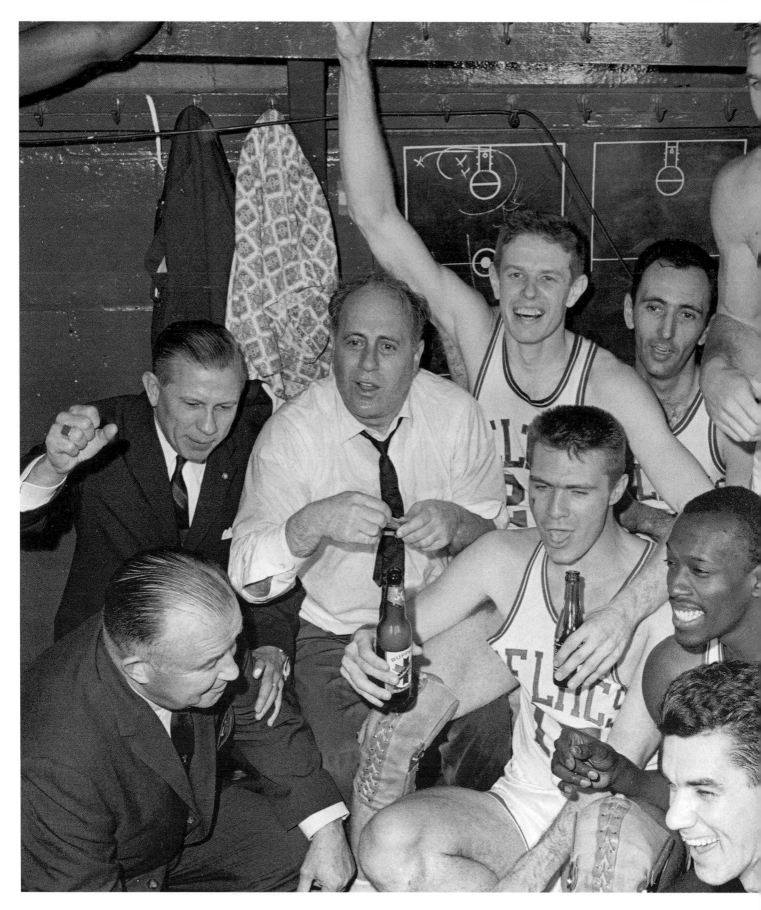

Above: *The Celtics celebrate their 1962 NBA title, a scene that was repeated nine times – including eight straight – under Red Auerbach.*

tion to tour the White House. While they were there, President John F. Kennedy, a Bostonian and rabid Celtics fan, learned of their presence, and he quickly carved a half hour out of his schedule to visit with them. When the visit ended, each player stopped on the way out of the Oval Office to shake hands with the President and say a few words. Satch was the last in line, and was extremely nervous about what he should say to Kennedy. When the moment arrived and he was shaking hands with the President, out came the immortal: "Take it easy, baby." The President broke up with laughter, and so did Auerbach and the Celtics. That became the team's slogan for a

would then negotiate, and when Satch felt the figure represented what he should be paid, he flipped the sign so it read: "Okay, I'll take it."

That was also the Celtics' reaction after the 1962 NBA playoffs in which they were pushed to a pair of seven-game series after winning a record 60 regular-season games. First they beat the Philadelphia Warriors and Chamberlain for the conference title in a very physical series, particularly in the fifth game when Philadelphia's Guy Rodgers grabbed a wooden photographer's stool to defend himself while scurrying across the Garden floor to escape an enraged Loscutoff. Sam Jones had done the same when Chamberlain went after him. "If I'm going to fight him, it wasn't going to be a fair fight on my part," Jones later said. The series came down to the final two seconds of the seventh game when Sam Jones's 18-footer from his "sweet spot" gave the Celtics a 109-107 lead. The Warriors tried an alley-oop inbounds pass to Chamberlain, but Russell outleaped him and swatted the ball to Sam Jones.

The Celtics then played the Los Angeles Lakers and came within a eyelash of seeing the end of their four-year title run in the

Below: *The Celtics and Lakers met six times for the NBA title during the 1960s, and Boston won each time. Here, K. C. Jones (25) battles Gene Wiley for the ball in the 1962 finals.*

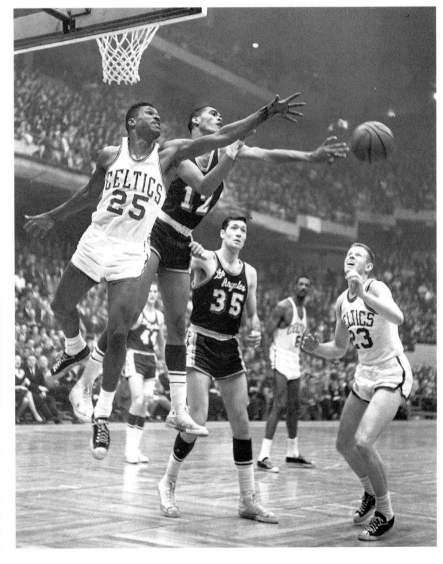

long time, as it did around the Oval Office.

Sanders also never looked forward to negotiating his contract with Auerbach (nor did any of the other Celtics, who often used to drop them on Walter Brown's desk and allow him to fill in the amount), and he would walk into Red's office holding up a sign that read: "It's not enough." The two

Above: *Bob Cousy tosses up a shot against Cincinnati in the 1963 playoffs at Boston Garden, where the Celtics were all but invincible as they won 68 of 89 playoff games during their dynasty run, including four seventh-game title victories.*

final two seconds of the seventh game. Early in the series, Sanders did a superlative job of guarding Baylor, and still he scored 61 points in a 126-121 victory at Boston Garden. That sent Los Angeles home with a 3-2 series edge, but the Celtics beat them, 119-105, on the West Coast to force the dramatic seventh game in Boston. There have been few moments in Celtics history to match the excitement of the final seconds of this game or the offensive maneuvering of this wild-and-woolly series.

Frank Selvy, who once scored 100 points for Furman University, was now a point guard for the Lakers, and his job was to feed Jerry West and Baylor. Yet in game seven it was he who had brought the Lakers to the brink of a great upset with two clutch baskets that forced a 100-100 tie. The Lakers had the ball with five seconds to play and called time out to set up the final play, in which Baylor and Rudy LaRusso set picks to free up West or Selvy for the shot. Selvy inbounded the ball to Rod Hundley, and then quickly moved into position to get a return pass and a possible shot. Hundley looked first for West, the Lakers' best scorer, but K. C. Jones had him completely tied up. He then found Selvy wide open and with two seconds on the clock Selvy went for a 19-foot jump shot. The ball bounced from rim to rim before it fell into Russell's hands, and the clock ran out.

Early in the overtime, Ramsey became the fourth Celtics player to foul out trying to cover Baylor, whose constant head-bobbing disconcerted every defender and seemed to give him a slight edge with his endless variety of shots. Ramsey played with a left thigh so badly swollen that it had to be tightly wrapped, and when not playing he sprinted up and down the corridors of the Garden so his leg would not tighten up. Still, he scored 23 points, including 15 of 16 foul shots, before being replaced by Gene Guarilia.

Guarilia, like all of Auerbach's role players, did his job magnificently over the next two minutes, using his unusually long arms to deflect a couple of Baylor's shots before harassing him into committing a sixth personal foul.

Sam Jones and Russell had taken command by this time: Jones scored five of his 27 points in overtime and Russell had played all 53 minutes, scoring 30 points and grabbing 40 rebounds in a performance that stunned West, who saw him sagging and limp on the Celtics' bench before the start of overtime. Cousy then capped the win by dribbling out the clock's final 20 seconds.

The heroics in that series proved that, if nothing else, the Celtics had a flair for the dramatic. Thus it was that Cousy, who announced before the start of the 1962-63 season that he was retiring, was properly saluted and toasted everywhere he played that season. He had been the preeminent guard of his time – and still is considered one of the greatest ever to play the game – but already his successor for this honor was in place in Cincinnati in the form of Oscar Robinson. The Big O helped the Royals into the playoffs where they took the Celtics to seven games before Cousy's 21 points and 11 assists inspired the Celtics to a 142-131 seventh-game victory.

Back came the Los Angeles Lakers for a second straight year, and Cousy saved the best part of his final year to help the Celtics to their fourth straight NBA title. Boston, up three games to two, held a nine-point lead early in the fourth quarter when Cousy tore the ligaments in his left foot. After he hobbled off the court, Los Angeles quickly shaved the Celtics' lead to just one point. Trainer Buddy Leroux had frozen the affected area, and strapped it up sufficiently to allow Cousy some mobility, and that's all he needed. With 4:43 to play, he re-entered the game and guided his team to a 112-109 victory, fittingly dribbling the ball during the final seconds before heaving it to the top of the rafters of the Los Angeles Sports Arena.

The man who had helped trigger all of those victories and championships had made one last statement – Celtics style.

Above: *Saying goodbye to the Celtics was difficult for Bob Cousy when he retired after the 1963 season. His 6,949 assists are still a team record.*

Left: *Cousy's retired jersey number 14, and Ed Macauley's number 22, hang from the rafters of Boston Garden, the Valhalla of Celtics heroes.*

5. A New Cast, Same Dynasty

Below: *Clyde Lovellette renewed his fading career with the Celtics as a valuable "role player" in the mid-1960s.*

Below right: *John Havlicek (17) tried pro football with the Cleveland Browns before joining the Celtics in 1962.*

With Bill Sharman and Bob Cousy retired, the Celtics dynasty gradually began to take on a new look during the 1960s, but with the exception of the 1966-67 season the results always were the same – an NBA championship. Coach Red Auerbach, the Master Builder, knew that he had not only put together a great basketball team of highly skilled players, but also a delicate human mechanism whose parts relied for their success on a group feeling that became known as "Celtics Pride."

When he assumed his role as Red Auerbach, the Master Rebuilder, he knew that the balance that had driven the team to six NBA titles in seven seasons could not easily be replaced, so he deliberately took a cautious course. As long as older players were productive and stayed in the spirit of the team, he kept them on, ignoring all of the whisperings about his team getting "too old." Age was a relative factor, he told his critics, because some players were physically and mentally younger than their years.

When Auerbach gradually rebuilt his teams, he did so through the player draft and by trading for experienced players who

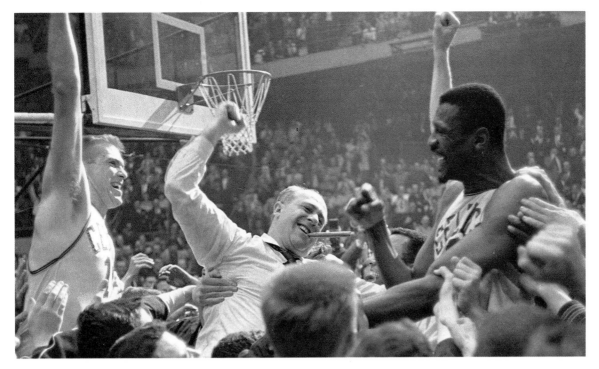

Left: *Red Auerbach, victory cigar firmly in place, joins Tom Heinsohn (left) and Bill Russell for a victory ride in 1964 after the Celtics became the first pro team ever to win six consecutive championships.*

could play mistake-free and could accept new roles on the team. That is why, as players such as Tom Heinsohn, Jim Loscutoff, Gene Guarilia and Frank Ramsey retired, he deftly acquired veteran players that other teams considered washed up – among them Clyde Lovellette and Johnny McCarthy from the St. Louis Hawks, Don Nelson from the Lakers, Wayne Embry from the Royals, Willie Naulls from the New York Knicks, and Bailey Howell from the Baltimore Bullets.

He was successful with this technique for two reasons: those veteran players longed to play on a championship team after being frustrated for many seasons; and they were older players who knew their limitations and could adjust to become role players if it meant gaining that long-sought title.

As these new faces appeared one by one from 1963 to 1968, Auerbach the Master Mixer blended them with the dwindling remnants of his great teams – Bill Russell, K. C. and Sam Jones, John Havlicek and Tom Sanders. When the 1964 season began, Havlicek certainly was no proven quantity, and many wondered whether the Celtics could survive the loss of Cousy. Auerbach had bulwarked his team by obtaining Naulls and Lovellette to spell Russell – a bit of irony because one of the few serious physical altercations in which Russell was ever involved had been against Lovellette several seasons earlier.

Havlicek's Ohio State teammate and close friend, Larry Siegfried, who had played in the American Basketball League following graduation, also joined the team. Siggy got the job done any way he could – by diving after loose balls, harassing opponents, and generally flying around the court trying to disrupt offenses and defenses. He was never pretty and often looked totally out of control, and he always stirred things up. When Russell became a player-coach for the final three years of his career, he would often turn to Siegfried for advice. When Siggy was on the bench he would share with Russell his perceptions about the direction of the game.

K. C. Jones replaced Cousy as a starter in the Celtics' back court in the 1964 season and the team never skipped a beat. Part of the reason was the nucleus of talent still available, as well as the Celtics' quiet determination to show everyone that they were not a one-man team, and that Cousy's loss, as many had predicted, would not affect their title chances. And they proved just that as the team won 59 games – one short of the previous high – and became the first professional team ever to win six consecutive titles.

This team did it with defense, shifting to a pressure mode that suited the talents of Russell and K. C. Jones, and taking advantage of younger players such as Havlicek and Sanders, who were able to sustain this tough style of play over longer periods of time.

Russell also thrived, free at last from the imposing shadow of Cousy that had somewhat diminished his achievements in the minds and hearts of New England fans during the previous seven seasons. He had his best rebounding season ever with 1,950 (an average of 25 per game), and the Celtics roared through the playoffs, defeating both Cincinnati and the San Francisco Warriors (the Philadelphia Warriors with Wilt Chamberlain had moved west in 1962) with a pair of 4-1 series wins.

That marked the end for Ramsey and Loscutoff, but the Celtics didn't even blink, except to mourn the loss of owner Walter Brown, who died shortly before the start of the 1964-65 season. They dedicated the season to him, just as they had dedicated the previous season to proving their abilities without Cousy. It was as if the team needed a special cause to ward off the twin evils associated with repetitious success – boredom and lack of motivation. It worked; the team roared to a 31-7 start and set an NBA record with 62 victories.

The Cincinnati Royals had emerged as one of the team's principal Eastern Division challengers with such great players as Oscar Robertson, Jerry Lucas, Wayne Embry and Jack Twyman. The new Philadelphia 76ers rose to the challenge as well, with Wilt Chamberlain on their roster. Thus it was that the Celtics-Chamberlain confrontation was joined for the fourth time in six seasons, and like most of the others this one went right down to the seventh game for the divisional championship. The Celtics blew an early 18-point margin, and led by a point at the half. Auerbach turned up the heat in the second half and Boston relentlessly battled to a comfortable lead. With a minute to play, the Celtics were ahead, 110-103, and Auerbach lit up one of his patented victory cigars while sold-out Boston Garden went crazy.

Then, so did the game – and from a jubilant victory party, that final minute turned into a horror show. The Celtics didn't press the 76ers and Chamberlain rattled off six quick points, the final two on a thunderous dunk with just five seconds to play, cutting Boston's once-safe lead to just one point. Sensing they still had an opportunity to win, the 76ers pressed Russell so fiercely as he tried to inbound the ball that he finally jumped into the air and threw it. But in doing so, his pass hit a wire that helped secure the basket to the Garden's balcony, and the ball bounced backward. Philadelphia's ball!

A stunned Russell, who never had made such a critical mistake, came to the Boston bench pleading for someone to "make a big play and take me off the hook."

Ironically, before the game, Auerbach and 76ers Coach Dolph Schayes had discussed the lower-than-usual position of the wires. Schayes wanted a team to retain possession of the ball should an inbounds pass strike them. Auerbach demurred, noting the ground rule at the Garden had always stipulated the other team got possession. The memory of that discussion was sharpened by the sudden, cold reality of having to give up the ball in the shadow of its own basket, with enough time for the

76ers to win the title. Anyone who watched the game will remember the image of a crushed Heinsohn sitting on his team's bench, his head buried in his hands as the 76ers and Celtics plotted their final moves.

The Celtics' plan was simple: If the ball came in to Chamberlain, foul him immediately because he was such a poor foul shooter and had already missed eight free throws in that game. Otherwise, they had to play against whoever got the ball, and figure it would get to Chamberlain.

On the other hand, the 76ers had the option of going directly to Chamberlain; or to Hal Greer, their best outside shooter; or to Chet Walker, their second-best scorer, who could either pass it to Wilt or Greer, or drive to the basket himself. Coach Schayes chose the third option, with Greer inbounding the ball to Walker on the outside and then stepping behind a pick that Johnny Kerr would set on K. C. Jones near the corner. Greer would then take a return pass from Walker and shoot. Chamberlain and Luke Jackson were underneath for a possible rebound.

But the strategy never got started because Greer was pressed so badly trying to inbound the ball that he finally settled for a desperately thrown pass that arched lazily toward Walker. Havlicek, playing between Walker and Greer, had begun counting off the allotted five seconds to inbound a ball and when he reached three and nothing had happened, he turned quickly to check Walker's position, and then turned back in time to see Greer's soft pass. In an instant, he leaped and deflected the ball to Sam Jones as time expired.

Two persons in the Garden were forever immortalized in the single instant that the ball changed hands – John Havlicek and Celtics' radio broadcaster Johnny Most. Most had not yet achieved the legendary

Opposite: *The classic matchup: Bill Russell shoots while Wilt Chamberlain watches during the 1965 Eastern Division playoffs.*

Below: *The Celtics' seventh straight NBA title victory brought John Havlicek and Red Auerbach to the shoulders of the Boston Garden fans.*

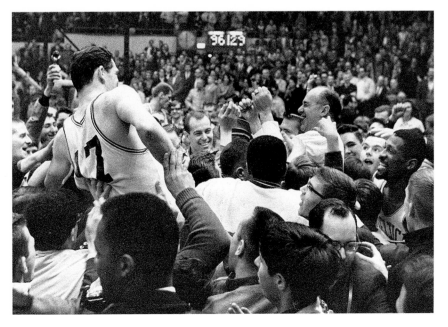

status that he would assume over the next two decades, but his description of that dramatic ending still is one of the great moments in the team's history. As Greer inbounded the ball, Most told his audience:

Greer is putting the ball in play. He gets it out deep . . . And Havlicek steals it! Over to Sam Jones. Havlicek stole the ball!

It's all over! It's all over! Johnny Havlicek is being mobbed by the fans! It's all over! Johnny Havlicek stole the ball! Oh boy, what a play by Havlicek at the end of this ball game! Johnny Havlicek stole the ball on the pass-in! Oh, my, what a play by Havlicek! A spectacular series comes to an end in spectacular fashion!

John Havlicek is being hoisted aloft. He raises his hand. Bill Russell wants to grab Havlicek. He hugs him! He squeezes John

Above: *Johnny Most (right, shirtsleeves) was the Celtics' "voice" for nearly 40 years, and his distinctive play-by-plays were legendary.*

Right: *John Havlicek made hundreds of great plays for the Celtics, but he is forever remembered for Johnny Most's famous "Havlicek Stole the Ball" description in the 1965 playoffs against the 76ers.*

Left: *John Havlicek, his arm raised in triumph as the Celtics near their seventh straight world title in 1965, was a valuable player for Red Auerbach as the famed "sixth man" before becoming a starter after Auerbach retired.*

Havlicek! Havlicek saved this ball game! Believe that! Johnny Havlicek saved the ball game. The Celtics win it, 110 to 109.

Most, who would become renowned for his gravelly voice and his rat-a-tat-tat broadcasting style, would build his legend on his immortal "Havlicek stole the ball!" sequence. No one worked himself into a bigger frenzy than Most in describing the Celtics' great plays, and Most had literally thousands of such moments during his career, which lasted from 1953 until 1989. Clips of Celtics games on evening New England TV newscasts often featured Most's radio play-by-play describing the action, because no sports anchor could even come close.

Most was a relentless smoker and coffee drinker during a game, and those who sat under his broadcasting position in the Garden were invariably subject to a coffee shower as his intensity level was punctuated with arm and hand swinging. Some even wore raincoats throughout the game to save cleaning bills. In Dallas one evening, he was almost thrown out of the arena for smoking, in violation of posted No Smoking signs. Two police officers escorted him to his broadcasting position to ensure that he obeyed the rule. Instead of starting his broadcast with his traditional "Johnny Most, high above courtside" routine, he went on the air by excoriating the Dallas police for allegedly ignoring crimes being committed throughout the area because "all the damn police care about is stopping Johnny Most from smoking. I hate Dallas."

And woe to the enemy player who played rough or unfairly. When a Celtics player once was thrown out of a game after elbow-ing an opponent in the eye, Most indignantly told his listeners it was "the worst bit of justice I have ever seen . . . the guy's eye struck his elbow, but our guy gets thrown out of the game!" He coined nicknames for two often overly aggressive Washington Bullets players, Jeff Ruland and Rick Mahorn, as "McFilthy & McNasty."

Then there was John Havlicek, the other person immortalized by that series-saving steal. Havlicek was number one draft pick of the Celtics after two All-America basketball seasons at Ohio State, where he helped the Buckeyes win the 1960 national championship, and finish second in two other appearances. When he had arrived at Ohio State and found the Bucks loaded with potential 20-points-per-night scorers like Jerry Lucas, Larry Siegfried, and Mel Nowell, he had decided against competing with them for the ball, and instead gained a reputation as one of college basketball's greatest defensive players. Yet, despite his achievements and top draft choice status, he opted to play professional football with the Cleveland Browns, who had made him a seventh-round draft pick in 1962, even though he had not played football since high school. When he reported to the Browns' training camp in July, he was placed at wide receiver and played in several exhibition games before being the final training camp cut. Pro football's loss became pro basketball's gain.

"John was a great athlete and I knew all about his football skills from my friends in East Liverpool, Ohio, where he had played," said Paul Brown, then coach of the Cleveland Browns, who had made the decision to draft him. "I sort of kept track of

Above: *Bill Russell helped Auerbach win his ninth NBA title in 1966 with a heart-stopping seventh game victory over the Lakers a few days after he had agreed to succeed him as head coach.*

him during his career at Ohio State, and Woody Hayes told us that he thought John had the athletic ability to make the swing. There was nothing wrong with his physical skills, but he didn't have the great speed that we required for our wide receivers. He also had to compete against Gary Collins, an All-America wide receiver from Maryland, our number one draft pick, who had great speed and the experience of college football. We also had a veteran team and that hurt his cause. Under those circumstances, I encouraged him to pursue his pro basketball career."

Havlicek's reputation for defensive excellence only increased when he joined the Celtics, and he soon earned the nickname "Spider" because it seemed as if he was all arms and legs. Of course, the great instincts and reflexes that helped make him a splendid defensive player served him equally well when he turned those same skills to becoming one of the greatest shooters in NBA history. Havlicek was not considered much of a scorer at first, but had to abide by

Auerbach's rule that a player take a shot if he was open and believed he could make it. Havlicek's instincts at first were to pass the ball, but once given the green light – like everything else that he did with such excellence during his career – he perfected his shooting. When he finally retired in 1978, he was the Celtics' all-time leading scorer – and second in NBA history behind Wilt Chamberlain!

Havlicek had succeeded Frank Ramsey as "sixth man," and no one ever did it better. John was absolutely indefatigable, a reputation he maintained during his entire 17-season career. When he came into the game to face tired players, he upped the tempo several notches and dared teammate and foe alike to keep up. He played the back court and front court with equal efficiency, and long after that heroic steal in the 1965 playoffs, he became one of the most beloved of all Celtics heroes.

The Celtics regrouped from that squeaker against Philadelphia and blitzed the Lakers in five games for their seventh straight NBA title, then they did it again in 1966. This time, though, matters were different. Auerbach had announced he would retire after the season because he could not take the physical toll placed upon him after Walter Brown's death. "I wanted to give everyone their last shot at me, and not make it look like I was picking my spot to walk away only after we had won everything."

But it wasn't as easy in 1966, because the Celtics had lost many of their greatest players, and some of the others were getting older. For the first time since 1956, the team finished second in the division, to Philadelphia and Chamberlain. That mattered little, though, because the Celtics, after going down 2-1 against Cincinnati in the best-of-five first round, won the next two games, and then blew away the 76ers in five games to win the division crown.

For the fourth time in five seasons, Boston played the Lakers for the title, but unlike the previous year, this series went seven games – and almost ended in disaster for Auerbach and his team. As had happened the previous year against Philadelphia, it looked as if the Celtics would have another easy, happy ending, and everyone awaited the moment when the coach would light up his victory cigar. Russell's stuff shot gave Boston a 10-point lead with 30

seconds to play and the Garden crowd began to jam the endlines, ready to be a part of the game-ending celebrations. Jerry West scored two baskets, but still the Celtics led by six points with 14 seconds to play and Auerbach gave the crowd what it wanted. He leaned back and lit his cigar.

That sent a false signal to the crowd, which swarmed on to the court, engulfing some players and even mobbing Auerbach. Havlicek had to call time out because he couldn't get the ball into play, and it took pleas from Auerbach, the players and the public address announcer to clear the court. Worse yet, the Celtics also had come unglued, and turned the ball over four times in the next 10 seconds. Los Angeles closed to 95-93 with six seconds to play.

The roar that had engulfed the Garden just moments before became a deathly hush until K. C. Jones got the inbounds pass and dribbled out the final seconds. Auerbach left the Garden floor after his final game atop the shoulders of his delirious partisans, but noted ruefully later, "I never came closer to disaster" than in the moments that followed the final victory cigar.

He also walked away with his 885th win as head coach, but he wasn't through. As general manager and president, Auerbach would guide the team through three more decades of Celtics basketball.

Below left: *No one enjoyed winning more than Red Auerbach. Here, he delights in a late-game Celtics basket that would bring him his seventh consecutive world championship, in 1965.*

Below: *John Havlicek scored more points and played more minutes than anyone in Celtics history.*

6. Russell Conducts The Dynasty

Eleven days before the Celtics won their ninth NBA championship in 1966, Red Auerbach announced that Bill Russell would succeed him as head coach the next season, and would continue to play. It was the first time in the modern sports era that a black man had been named as head coach of a professional team, and while that was one of the noble gestures involved in the move, it was not the big reason. Bill Russell himself was the big reason.

When Auerbach decided that he was going to retire after the 1966 season, his first choices for coach were former players such as Bob Cousy, then head coach at Boston College; Frank Ramsey; and Tom Heinsohn, who had just retired the previous spring. During lunch with Heinsohn early in the fall of 1965, he tossed out the names

and Tommy took himself out of the running, citing a growing and prosperous insurance business, but also candidly noting that he did not think that anyone could coach Russell. "The only one who can handle Russell is Russell," Heinsohn said. "Why not ask him?"

It made sense to Auerbach. He believed that Russell could coach and still play at the same time, getting appropriate help from someone on the bench to keep tabs on the game's pace, a role that Siegfried would play.

Auerbach knew that coaching changes also brought personality changes to a team, but he believed that Russell was still such a driving force that the players would follow his dictates. He also knew that the overall philosophy of the team would remain relatively unchanged, and being the wily old

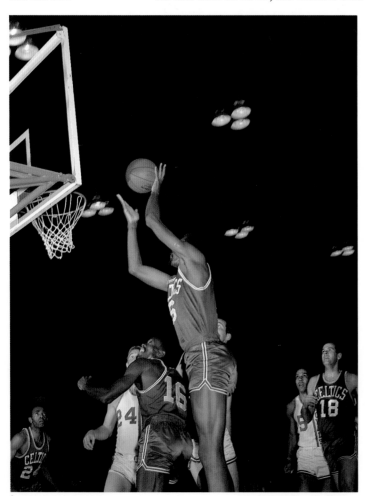

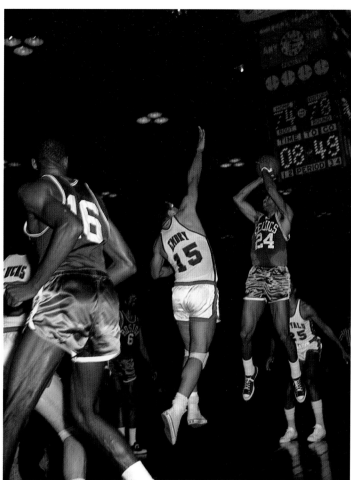

psychologist that he was, he felt that this also boded well for keeping its winning habits intact.

He was correct – the team won 60 games in Russell's first season, with a cast of characters that included newcomers Don Nelson, Bailey Howell and Wayne Embry. Nelson and Howell were very similar in their styles; they were both good shooters close to the basket, hard workers, adequate rebounders and very dedicated to success. Nellie came to the Celtics early in the 1965-66 season after stints at Chicago and Los Angeles, where he had been released. But Auerbach had seen enough of him in rare appearances to feel that he was the perfect Celtics player – someone who would go all out for as long as he was asked. Howell had played for seven seasons at Detroit and Baltimore and was a tireless rebounder, averaging nearly 10 a game, which when playing with Russell was a good night's work.

Wayne Embry had been one of the NBA's finest centers for the eight seasons he had played with the Cincinnati Royals, and he waged some tremendous battles with Russell. At 6-feet, 8-inches tall and 255 pounds, Wayne was a great physical force under the basket (he was nicknamed "The Wall"), and the Celtics didn't lose all that much whenever he spelled Russell. He was considering retirement in 1966 when Auerbach con-

vinced him to end his career in Boston. Embry still maintains that his decision to join the Celtics was the best one he ever made as a basketball player. It was just as good for the Celtics because, like Nelson and Howell, Embry brought the kind of experience, spirit and outlook to the team that helped make Auerbach's transition to the front office much smoother and worry-free.

While these new faces blended into the Celtics' style, which had tempered its wide-open style of basketball to settle for a more geriatric style of halfcourt offense, there was no stopping Wilt Chamberlain and the 76ers, and they roared their way through the season to the NBA championship, eliminating the Celtics in five games – the only time that Russell ever lost to a Chamberlain-led team in the playoffs.

The Celtics also had come to the conclusion that winning the Eastern Division championship was nice, but not necessary. The pragmatist in Auerbach figured it was better to get into the playoffs by whatever means possible, and then gear up everyone's enthusiasm, talent and, most of all, mental and physical stamina for a 19-game run to the NBA title. Why wear out Russell and the other veteran players for the sake of winning a division title, when all that might bring is playoff elimination?

So for the next two seasons, the Celtics

Above left: *K. C. Jones was a tenacious competitor who very quietly became a key player during the Celtics' dynasty.*

Above: *Sam Jones (24) was unheralded when he reported to the Celtics from North Carolina College in 1957. He became the highest scoring guard in the team's history.*

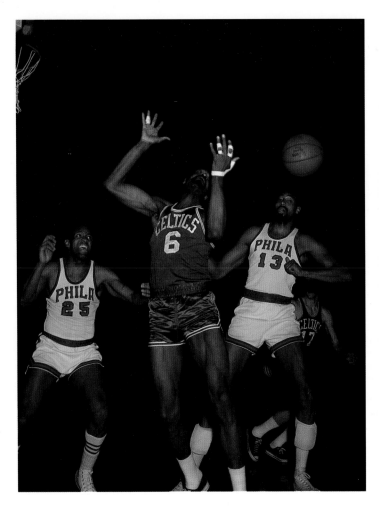

Above: *Bill Russell didn't always win the statistical battle against Wilt Chamberlain, but he was the overall victor with his 11 NBA titles.*

Above right: *Bailey Howell, John Havlicek and Larry Siegfried battle the 76ers' Wilt Chamberlain in the 1968 Eastern Division playoffs, in which the Celts came from a 3-1 deficit to win the title.*

were always competitive but they were not the division's best team. In 1967-68, they again finished second to the 76ers, then roared from a 1-2 deficit to three straight wins in their opening series against Detroit before Russell scrapped Havlicek's sixth-man role and made him a starter.

But all the energy they apparently had saved seemed to be for naught when the 76ers zoomed to a 3-1 lead in the division championship series. Boston had shocked the favored champs by winning the first game of the series 127-118 in Philadelphia on an emotion-packed day following the assassination of civil rights leader Dr. Martin Luther King, Jr. The NBA then stopped its playoff schedule until after Dr. King's funeral, by which time the Celtics' momentum from that first victory had disappeared, and 10 days later the team was back in Philadelphia and on the brink of elimination.

Chamberlain, with Luke Jackson, Chet Walker, Hal Greer and Wali Jones – and egged on by a packed Spectrum crowd of more than 15,000 – brimmed with a smugness that advertised their intention of rubbing out their chief tormentors for a second straight season. But it didn't happen, because Russell turned up his game a notch, and everyone followed. Four days later, the two teams faced each other again in the Spectrum with the series tied at

three games and the 76ers and their followers not quite so smug.

When it was over Boston came away with one of the greatest triumphs in its history with a gritty 100-96 victory, the first NBA team ever to come from a 3-1 deficit and win a championship. Chamberlain, who had tried to emulate Russell and concentrate his efforts on rebounding and assists, shot only twice in the second half and scored just 14 points overall to make Boston's defensive chores much easier.

When Russell was convinced that Wilt wasn't interested in scoring in the second half, he moved Embry to guard him. Wayne was strong enough to keep Wilt from muscling his way toward the basket. Russell then guarded Jackson and prevented him from getting off any easy shots when the 76ers desperately tried to make a run late in the fourth quarter.

In the bedlam of the victorious Celtics' locker room after the game, someone gushingly asked Sam Jones to explain what really was the key to such a dramatic comeback. "Oh, man," Sam said with a laugh, "it was the money."

But it was a lot more, because every Celtic who got into the game contributed – seven of the eight players hit double figures, with Embry, Havlicek and Jones scoring 63 points among them. The eighth player, Tom Thacker, played his role in the

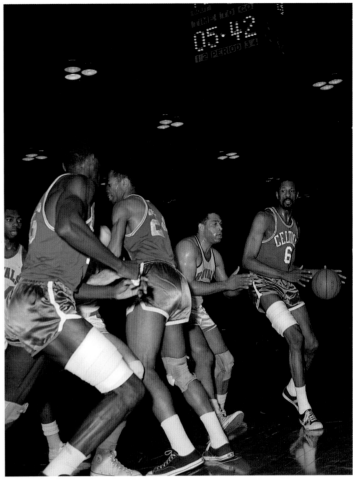

final minutes by taking four fouls to disrupt the 76ers' comeback attempt.

Six games later against the Lakers, Boston won the NBA championship, after splitting the first four games, completely overmatching the Western Division champs in every phase of the game. Havlicek capped the 124-109 final game victory with 40 points.

It seemed only fitting that the last season of the 1960s, which was so magnificently ruled by the Celtics, should also be the final year of its dynasty. Sam Jones had announced that he was retiring after the season and Russell had made up his mind to do likewise. The Eastern Division had shifted dramatically. Dogged by a continual string of injuries and advancing years, the Celtics finished fourth, their worst since 1955. Philadelphia had tired of Chamberlain's mercurial personality and traded him to the Los Angeles Lakers, and the 76ers fell behind Baltimore, which won the division title behind rookie Wes Unseld and the New York Knicks. The Knicks had emerged from nearly two decades of mediocrity and were on the brink of their early 1970s title runs with such players as Jerry Lucas, Willis Reed, Bill Bradley, Dave DeBusschere and Walt Frazier. At the same time, a juicy rivalry had emerged between the Celtics and Knicks that was fueled in part by thousands of young New York college students in Boston, who bought every available Garden seat.

But the injuries that had hampered the Celtics throughout the season disappeared when the playoffs began as Boston easily polished off the 76ers in five games and the Knicks, with Auerbach fuming and bristling at the noisy incursion of the young Knicks fans, in six games.

All the so-called experts, who had written off Boston for the third straight year, smugly assured everyone that they "would get theirs" against the Lakers, with Wilt Chamberlain, Elgin Baylor and Jerry West. The Lakers believed it too, after winning the first two games in Los Angeles, since the Celtics couldn't match their firepower. Los Angeles was so sure it could end the series in four games that cases of champagne accompanied their basketball gear to Boston. Bad guess, because the two teams – and the Lakers' champagne – returned to the West Coast five days later, tied at two games apiece. Boston had narrowly won the fourth game when L.A. blew a one-point lead in the final 15 seconds after Emmette Bryant stole the ball, and Sam Jones tossed up a shot that barely fell in to give Boston a gritty 89-88 victory.

The Lakers regained the lead with an easy 117-104 victory in game five, and the teams – with the Lakers' champagne again in tow – returned to Boston. But the Celtics

Above left: *John Havlicek and Don Nelson (19) were two valuable players during the Celtics' transition from the Russell era to the 1970s, where they continued to win NBA titles.*

Above: *In a game against Cincinnati, Bill Russell works against future teammate Wayne Embry as Sam Jones and Tom Sanders set picks. Embry later helped Boston to win the 1968 NBA title.*

Opposite: *John Havlicek was a defensive specialist at Ohio State, but became such a great all-around NBA player that he led the Celts in scoring in nine straight years and in assists for six straight seasons.*

Right: *Bill Russell yanks down one of his 21,620 lifetime rebounds. He holds the club record of 51 for one game, against Syracuse in 1960, and twice had 49, against Philadelphia and Detroit.*

were undaunted and turned up the defensive pressure to win, 99-90. Still the Lakers were so certain they could win the title that for the seventh game at The Forum, owner Jack Kent Cooke ordered thousands of balloons secured in the rafters; had the 300-piece University of Southern California marching band tuned up to lead a noisy celebration; and that well-traveled champagne iced and ready to open. However, someone forgot the tell Russell and the Celtics, and in one last, mighty effort, he and his Over-the-Hill Gang riddled the Lakers for three quarters. They held a three-point halftime lead, and in the third quarter their defense choked off the Lakers' offense without a point for a five-minute burst, during which time Boston had an 11-point run. They held a commanding 17-point advantage going into the final period. But the Lakers came back, helped by the fatigue that was by then numbing the Celtics' players, fifth fouls on Russell and Havlicek, and the hot shooting hand of Jerry West.

Then came one of the game's two key plays. With Boston leading 103-94, Chamberlain grabbed a rebound and injured his right knee. He hobbled around the court for a couple of plays and then took himself out of the game – to the disapproval of his coach, Bill van Breda Kolff – with

Boston ahead by seven points and 5:19 to play. Ex-Celtic Mel Counts replaced him and helped by West, the Lakers carved the lead to 103-102 with 3:07 to play. Wilt motioned that he wanted to return, but Van Breda Kolff ignored him.

The second big play occurred with 77 seconds to play when Havlicek had the ball deflected out of his hands by Keith Erickson with the shot clock running out. The ball went to Don Nelson at the foul line and his desperation clock-beating shot hit the rim, bounced straight up and back down through the basket for one of the most improbable scores in Celtics history – and a 105-102 lead. Larry Siegfried's two fouls nailed down matters, and moments later Russell went leaping and bounding off the court, followed by his victorious team that had just carved out a 108-106 victory.

A few minutes later, the Lakers in their locker room could hear Russell cackling and the Boston players celebrating – but not with any champagne. That still was in boxes – unopened.

Still, it was the only way to end the most fabulous run of success – 11 championships in 13 years – that any team had ever accomplished. There were no frills, no balloons, no marching bands, no bubbly. Just hard work and solid team play, the Celtics way.

7. David vs. the NBA's Goliath

Tom Heinsohn was named to succeed Bill Russell as the Celtics' head coach before the start of the 1970 season. During the next eight seasons he did a coaching job that many believe was on a par with Red Auerbach's coaching during his first five seasons. Heinsohn concentrated on rebuilding and retooling the rundown Celtics, and made them the scourge of the NBA for most of his tenure. Both Auerbach and Heinsohn knew from the outset it was going to be a struggle because, while many of the integral parts of the Celtics' dynasty – John Havlicek, Don Nelson, Satch Sanders, Bailey Howell and Larry Siegfried – returned, there was no one to replace the most important one: Bill Russell.

The Celtics tried, getting 7-foot Henry Finkel from San Diego. Though he later became one of the most beloved of all Celtics role players during two NBA championship

seasons, Finkel was a target of criticism as Boston sank to a 34-48 record the season after Russell departed. Heinsohn, another target, quickly realized that the team was not going to win anything, so he began rebuilding for the future, helped by the draft of All-America guard Jo-Jo White from Kansas to go with Don Chaney, a top pick in Russell's final season, and forward Steve Kuberski. But the biggest building block came the next season with top pick Dave Cowens, a 6-foot, 8½-inch center from Florida State University.

All of the so-called experts agreed that Cowens was too small to play center in the NBA, but none of them looked past his physical statistics and into his heart. In fact, he was, as Celtics scout Mal Graham declared, "the best jumping white man I ever saw," which meant he played much bigger than his frame, much as Russell's

Below: *Jo-Jo White, an All-America at Kansas, filled the role of the shooting guard on two Celts NBA title teams.*

Below right: *Tom Heinsohn totally rebuilt the Celtics after the Russell era, winning NBA titles in 1974 and 1976.*

Left: *Dave Cowens made up for what he lacked in size with intensity and determination under the boards when he became the Celtics' center during the 1970s. He accumulated over 10,000 rebounds during his career, and was inducted into the Hall of Fame in 1991.*

great leaping ability allowed him to play far above his 6-foot, 10-inch frame.

But as much as any other contributing attributes, it was his high intensity and competitiveness that drove him to greatness. There never had been a more intense Celtics player. He dove for loose balls on the floor, sailed into the stands to save errant throws, and was a madcap leaper whose sharp elbows cleared space under the basket. He also had one great attribute around which Heinsohn fashioned a team that closely resembled the great Celtics teams on which he had played: Cowens could outrun any center in the league, which he did with abandon until his opponents dragged themselves, exhausted, off the floor. Cowens'

speed blended perfectly with the stamina of John Havlicek, the youth of Steve Kuberski, Jo-Jo White and Don Chaney, and the power of Don Nelson, Satch Sanders and another great acquisition a year later, power forward Paul Silas.

Heinsohn never asked Cowens to play above his capabilities, but instead fashioned an offense that forced the bigger opponents to change their games. Knowing that Cowens could not take a constant pounding under the basket, Heinsohn stationed him at the top of the key, where his very good jump shot was effective, and most importantly, where opposing centers had to come out and play him. That left the basket area open for "back door" plays and also

Above: *Paul Silas came to the Celtics from Phoenix in 1973 and filled the power forward position as well as anyone in the team's history during his three seasons. He averaged more than 12 rebounds a game and helped the team to a pair of NBA titles.*

that had become apparent the previous season when, with such players as Dave Debusschere, Bill Bradley and center Willis Reed, the New York Knicks had run roughshod over the Celtics' front line. Silas provided more than 1,000 rebounds a season and took much of the rebounding pressure off Cowens and Sanders. Cowens and Silas both finished among the league leaders during their four seasons together, and Silas became even more effective following his first season with the Celtics, when he filled the "sixth man" role in replacing Kuberski, Nelson and Sanders.

Heinsohn thus had in place a well-rounded team that ran off great bursts of offense. Nelson was effective under the boards; White had assumed a role once held by Sam Jones (even to wearing the same kind of leg wrap and shooting a soft, board-kissing jump shot); Sanders and Kuberski were aggressive rebounders abetted by Silas; and Chaney became a defensive back-court specialist while still honing his shooting stills.

Yet, Havlicek was the team's prime mover, reveling in the up-tempo game while providing the best on-the-court leadership and production the team had seen since Cousy's heyday. Even Cowens was amazed, noting one day, "I'm out there thinking about how fast I'm going and Havlicek comes roaring past, yelling, 'Come on, Dave, quit lagging!'"

All of this had begun to jell in 1972 when the team had three big winning streaks that equaled 36 victories in 42 games. Then they defeated Atlanta in six games in their first playoff action since Russell's final season, before losing to the Knicks in the conference finals. The team chemistry jelled even more the following year with the acquisition of Silas and rookie guard Paul Westphal, when Boston had a club record 68 victories that included streaks in which they won 43 of 45 games, and had an NBA record 32 road wins. Cowens had his best season with a 20.5 scoring average, 1,329 rebounds and 333 assists.

Still the Knicks, who finished 11 games behind Boston in the Atlantic Division, faced off with them again in the conference finals. In game four the Knicks pulled off a heart-thumping 117-110 double-overtime victory after the Celtics blew a 16-point lead in the final 10 minutes of regulation, and the New Yorkers took a commanding 3-1 lead. Havlicek had injured his shoulder in the previous game and did not play. Though he needed help to comb his hair, he gave a valiant effort before the team was finally eliminated, 94-78, in the seventh game, scoring the fewest playoff points of any Celtics team since 1954.

took advantage of Cowens's good passing ability to get the ball inside to Nelson, Sanders and Havlicek, for easier baskets.

When Cowens was matched against towering centers like Kareem Abdul-Jabbar, Bob Lanier and Wilt Chamberlain, Heinsohn made no great adjustments. Instead, he ordered Cowens to play as aggressively as he could against them without double-team help while the rest of the Celtics played tough defense. Thus, it didn't matter whether Abdul-Jabbar scored 44 points, because when the Celtics held his mates in check, the Celtics won.

All of this became easier to achieve when, before the 1973 season, Auerbach traded the rights to guard Charlie Scott, who was playing with the Virginia Squires of the American Basketball Association, to the Phoenix Suns for power forward Paul Silas. Silas was a six-season veteran who had not kept himself in good physical shape. But Auerbach put him on a 40-pound weight loss program, and Silas filled a dire need

All of that only served as a warm-up for two more NBA titles during the next three seasons. In 1974, helped by the acquisition of Westphal, Silas's move to sixth man and Nelson's role as a starter, the team rolled to a 29-6 record by mid-January, then defeated Buffalo and the Knicks in the conference playoffs, with Havlicek averaging 29 points a game against the Knicks.

The Celtics played the Milwaukee Bucks, which featured Abdul-Jabbar and Oscar Robertson, for the NBA title. Prospects looked good when Boston brought a 3-2 lead home to Boston Garden, but in one of the greatest NBA playoff games ever, the desperate Bucks rallied for a heart-stopping 102-101 double-overtime victory. Havlicek scored with five seconds to play in the first overtime to keep the game tied, then seemed to ice the win and the NBA title with a pair of last minute baskets (the second an almost blind, high-arching shot from the corner over a leaping Abdul-Jabbar with just eight seconds to play) for a 101-100 lead.

The Bucks called timeout and set up a play to Jon McGlocklin, but the Celtics pressured the ball so hard that the inbounds pass came to Abdul-Jabbar in the corner. In desperation, he uncorked one of his famed "sky hooks" and it fell through

Left: *John Havlicek flashes past Kareem Abdul-Jabbar to score during a memorable double overtime loss to Milwaukee in the 1974 finals. Boston won the series in seven games.*

Below: *Thousands of young collegians from New York bought seats at Boston Garden to rev up a fierce rivalry between the Knicks and Celtics in the early 1970s. The Celtics lost to them for the conference title in 1972 and 1973 before beating them in 1974.*

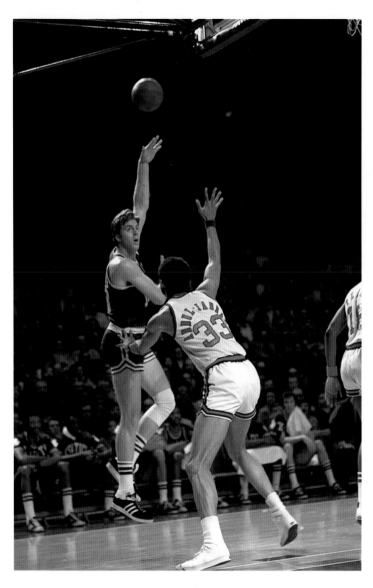

Above: *Dave Cowens forced bigger opposing centers such as Kareem Abdul-Jabbar to play him away from the basket because of his fine array of outside shots.*

Above right: *John Havlicek's off-balance shot forced a second overtime against the Bucks in the sixth game of the 1974 NBA finals.*

the basket, with three seconds to play, for the one-point win. There were no such heroics in the seventh game in Milwaukee when Boston held Abdul-Jabbar scoreless for nearly 18 minutes as Heinsohn altered his defensive strategy, moving Cowens in front of Jabbar, and Silas behind him. He gambled that the coverage would force the Bucks to kick the ball out to Cornell Warner, forcing him to shoulder an offensive load that was too great.

It worked! Warner scored just one point in 29 minutes and Boston led by as much as 17 points while Cowens had a 28-point, 14-rebound performance. The 102-87 victory secured the team's 12th NBA championship. That series also gained the team another important achievement – the Celtics finally were embraced forever by Boston. "For the first time, fans realized the magnitude of our championships," Auerbach said. "Until then, the Celtics were a household name all over the country – except in our own backyard. People just hadn't realized what they lost until it didn't happen for a couple of years, and helped by that double-overtime game and our coming back to win the championship, they finally

understood what the Celtics were about."

Those fans might have wondered a bit the following season, however; although the Celtics rolled to their fourth straight division title, winning 60 games and beating Atlanta in the first round of the playoffs, they were waxed by the Washington Bullets. Coached by former Celtic (and future Celtics coach) K. C. Jones, Washington defeated Boston in six games for the conference title. Heinsohn felt that the Celtics, who trailed badly in nearly every game, had expended so much energy crawling back from a huge deficit that they did not have enough steam left to sustain their advantage.

The Celtics learned their lesson well, as the 1976 team won its second NBA title in three seasons. While it was part of a deal that sent Charlie Scott to Phoenix that helped start this newest run of success, it was another deal that brought him *from* Phoenix – for Paul Westphal, who was unhappy with his salary situation – that sustained the run. Don Chaney played out his contract after another salary dispute, then joined St. Louis of the ABA. With those problems eradicated, the lethargy of the previous season was replaced by some newly found verve and the Celtics breezed to 54 wins despite not having any players among the NBA's top 20 scorers (although Cowens and Silas were among the top four rebounders).

In the playoffs the Celtics had some bad luck – Havlicek injured his foot and missed three games against Buffalo and played sparingly in two against Cleveland en route to the conference title. But they also had some good luck, in that three teams that might have overmatched them – Philadelphia, Washington and San Francisco – all were eliminated without having to play Boston. This brought the Celtics against the Phoenix Suns, winners of just 43 games, for the NBA title, and the stage was set for the most astounding Friday evening ever in Boston Garden.

That night, June 4, 1976, marked the most memorable game in Celtics history. It was a three-overtime thriller in which the Celtics finally outlasted the tenacious Suns 128-126, and during which occurred the most bizarre series of events ever to unfold during a Celtics game.

The Celtics had opened the series with two relatively easy wins over the Suns at the Garden, then were beaten two straight in Phoenix, setting up the pivotal fifth game at the Garden. Things seemed quite normal as the Celtics led 42-20 in the second quarter, and then 92-83 with 3:49 to play in the game. But the Westphal deal came back to haunt them as Paul led the Suns to a 95-95 tie at the end of regulation play by scoring nine of his team's final 11 points, including the last five. The teams played cautiously for most of the first two overtimes – each team scored six points in the first one – until Curtis Perry's jumper, following Westphal's steal, gave the Suns a one-point lead with only a few seconds to play in the second overtime.

Havlicek, who always thrived in such clutch situations, took the ball downcourt and sank a desperation, off-balance, 15-foot jump shot as the clock reached its final seconds for a 111-110 lead. Every one of the

Left: *Jo-Jo White scored more than 13,000 points and had over 3,600 assists, leading the Celtics for four consecutive seasons during his 10 years with the team. His jersey number 10 was retired in 1982.*

Above: *Don Nelson had been released by the Los Angeles Lakers in the early 1960s when the Celtics signed him, and he helped them to five NBA titles in 11 seasons.*

Right: *John Havlicek was still at the top of his game when he retired after his 16th season in 1978.*

Opposite: *Jo-Jo White perfected the same soft jumper that his predecessor Sam Jones had used so effectively.*

steamy conditions inside the antiquated arena. Still, the pace never slackened as White and two unlikely heroes – little-used Jim Ard, who replaced Cowens, and Glen McDonald, in for Silas – brought the Celtics to a victory in the final five minutes. Ard controlled a vital tip, and added two fouls, while McDonald scored six points and White added four of the 15 points he scored during the three overtimes. McDonald's baskets helped the Celtics put together a 126-120 lead, and Boston hung on for a 126-124 victory.

It almost seemed anticlimatic – except to Red Auerbach – that less than 36 hours later the Celtics clinched their 13th NBA title with an 87-80 victory in Phoenix. They used a 17-6 burst in the final seven minutes to clinch the win, which everyone seemed to relish even more because, as Auerbach noted, "We had to scratch and claw for everything." Heinsohn concurred, adding: "We never had our arsenal for the playoffs. We never knew what we could expect from Havlicek with his injured foot, and had to adjust from game to game. We got down to the last one and everyone poured his guts out. That's the only way we won."

It was simply another chapter in a long Celtics tradition.

15,520 fans in the Garden thought the Celtics had won because the clock ran out. But referee Richie Powers, the NBA's best, signaled that Phoenix had called a timeout with two seconds to play – even though they had exhausted their limit – and this touched off a melee. An enraged fan raced onto the court and punched Powers, and a near-riot ensued as other fans joined in, while police, and players from both teams, tried to restore order.

Westphal did it to his former team again because his heady timeout, while entitling Jo-Jo White to sink a technical foul shot for a 112-110 lead, allowed time-starved Phoenix to inbound the ball at midcourt instead of under their own basket. Garfield Heard got the inbounds pass, whirled and sank a 22-foot shot to tie the score 112-112 and force a third overtime.

Time and the brutal pace of play began to take its toll. Cowens, Scott and Silas all fouled out for Boston while the Suns lost center Alvin Adams and their other big man, Dennis Awtrey. On the Celtics' bench, Heinsohn, who had become renowned for his emotional displays during a game, was beginning to suffer from heat prostration from the pressures of the game and the

8. The Bird Era Takes Off

The secret to coping with the Celtics over the past four decades is simple: Never underestimate Red Auerbach. While other teams have sat around thinking up grandiose schemes, the wily Auerbach, relying on the single commodity called common sense – spiced with some foresight and more than a bit of chutzpah – made things happen.

For example, in the midst of the turmoil that surrounded the Celtics for two years after their 1976 championship, Auerbach came up with his second-best move ever: He chose forward Larry Bird of Indiana State University on the first round of the 1978 draft, even though Bird had another year of eligibility remaining.

Some two decades earlier, he had arranged his best-ever deal by maneuvering to draft Bill Russell, and while putting Bird's name on the draft list was not nearly as complicated, it nonetheless represented a considerable risk to the Celtics. Auerbach used the third pick of that draft – one the team desperately needed to upgrade itself immediately – to make the choice, knowing full well that Bird was going to stay in college that season and that he could lose him if Bird was unsigned before the next draft. This was a distinct possibility because he was certain to be the top pick in that draft, and might command even greater riches.

"I'll wait," Auerbach said with the calm that has always been his hallmark as a dealer. "I want Larry to enjoy his senior season, to play and get better, and then think about the Celtics when the season is over. I'm certain he'll want to join us."

And that's exactly how matters worked out – and with it came the second greatest player, behind Russell, in the team's history. The truth of the matter is that, as with Russell, Auerbach knew his prospect was a great player, but he never realized how great until, as with Russell, he began to play. Nor did he realize in the beginning that each of them would revolutionize the way in which the Celtics played the game, and cause their opponents to rewrite their books, as well.

Larry Bird was born to play basketball, and if he never does another thing for the rest of his life, he probably will have fulfilled his Creator's plan. Even as an untested NBA rookie, his basketball skills and instincts far exceeded those of any player extant – for which he also was paid some $3.5 million over five years (the most ever given to a rookie in pro sports to that time). The unusual thing about Bird is that he joined the special circle of great athletes that comprise the NBA's best players, even though he did not have great speed or jumping ability. But he didn't need those qualities to succeed because, with his ability to get good position and an uncanny instinct that told him precisely when to leap for a rebound, he held his own under the boards against bigger and stronger players. His moves down the court were always search-and-destroy missions; he was a marvelous passer who saw the entire court and then picked out the right player at the right moment with the right passing trajectory for scores. His own scoring touch was soon refined so that he was deadly from the three-point line right to the basket.

He also was a physical animal, who on a couple of occasions ran a five-kilometer

Below: *Red Auerbach's second biggest acquisition after Bill Russell was Larry Bird, whom he signed in 1979 for $3.5 million, the most ever paid to a rookie in pro sports.*

Left: *Larry Bird brought a complete set of basketball tools to the Celtics and helped them to three NBA titles before retiring in 1992.*

Left: *John Y. Brown's ownership of the Celtics in the late 1970s was such a disaster that Red Auerbach almost quit.*

charity race co-sponsored by the Celtics, and after crossing the finish line at Boston Garden, went inside and played nearly 48 minutes of basketball. One of his pre-game routines was to run a couple of miles around the arena's loge aisle, then shoot baskets for a couple of hours before his teammates arrived.

But Auerbach almost never got to realize the benefits of this great player. Since the death of Walter Brown, Red somehow had endured a succession of fly-by-night owners and still produced championship teams. But things got even worse when Irv Levin took control of the team, and a revolving door of player moves produced two horrible seasons in 1977 and 1978, causing Auerbach to have second thoughts about staying in Boston. In 1978 Levin and John Y. Brown, owner of the Buffalo Braves, swapped franchises so Levin could move his

Right: *John Y. Brown traded three number one draft picks for Bob McAdoo (11), a great scorer but not a player in the unselfish mold of the Celtics, because Phyllis George, a former Miss America and Brown's future wife, liked to watch him play.*

team to his native San Diego. Brown was a meddler who did not care for Auerbach's basketball acumen. Matters finally boiled over when he traded away three number one picks that Red had been hoarding to rebuild the team, for Bob McAdoo, a distinctly non-Celtics type of player. The deal was made on the whim of Brown's future wife, former Miss America Phyllis George, who had enjoyed watching McAdoo play for the Knicks.

That convinced Auerbach that he could not co-exist with Brown, and he began negotiating with those same Knicks to become their chief operating officer. Negotiations had reached the point that Red was en route by cab to the airport to fly to New York to consummate the deal, when his taxi driver made such a plaintive plea for him to stay – abetted by some common sense advice Auerbach had already heard from his wife – that he junked the idea, and

stayed to build another great team.

He was helped when Brown left to pursue a gubernatorial campaign in his native Kentucky, and sold his ownership share to Harry Mangurian. Finally, Auerbach worked for an owner who had deep pockets and a willingness to allow him to run the team without interference – and run it he did, right into three more NBA titles during the 1980s.

His first move was to sign Bill Fitch as head coach for the 1980 season to replace player-coach Dave Cowens, who had begun to struggle with the mental burdens of the game. That was Cowens's last season because, believing his physical skills were eroding and that he no longer was earning his keep at age 34, he stunned everyone by retiring early in the 1981 season. His final legacy was passing on to Bird the unique Celtics leadership mantle – the same one that had been given to him by John Havlicek and Don Nelson – which Bird then passed on to the players who formed the great teams of the 1980s.

Bill Fitch was a hard-working, wisecracking coach who had guided the Cleveland Cavaliers from expansion status to playoff capability; he was just the type of coach Auerbach wanted to mold his emerging team. Fitch rose to the challenge by taking the Celtics to five playoffs and the 1981 NBA title.

Bird, of course, was the linchpin. He joined the team for the 1979-80 season, and with Dave Cowens, Cedric "Cornbread" Maxwell, Rick Robey, Chris Ford, Tiny Archibald and M. L. Carr, ripped off a league-leading 61 victories, a 22-game turnaround from the previous season that was the biggest in NBA history. Boston won the division title and made it to the Eastern Conference finals before losing to Philadelphia. Maxwell, a number one pick in 1977, was a superb inside player in the mold of Don Nelson, and he helped the team to titles in 1981 and 1984. He scored more than 8,000 points and grabbed more than 4,000 rebounds during his eight seasons with Boston.

In 1980 the Celtics had the top draft pick, which they had obtained from Detroit as part of a deal that sent McAdoo to the Pistons as compensation for signing free agent M. L. Carr. Carr later became the Celtics' spiritual leader for three championship seasons. In the meantime, wanting to add some height to his team, Auerbach

Above left: *In a desperate quest to revive the team during the 1979 season, Dave Cowens was named head coach. Bill Fitch replaced him the next season.*

Above: *Nate (Tiny) Archibald ran the Celtics offense during the 1978-83 seasons and accumulated more than 2,500 assists en route to the Hall of Fame.*

Above: *K. C. Jones became head coach in 1984 and immediately brought the Celtics their 15th NBA title. He added another in 1986 and won 308 games in five seasons.*

Above right: *Cedric (Cornbread) Maxwell was the Celtics' number one draft pick in 1977. His famous cry of "jump on my back" helped the Celtics to win the 1984 NBA title in a seventh-game showdown against the Lakers.*

engineered a deal in which he traded top pick in the 1980 draft to the Golden State Warriors for 7-foot center Robert Parish, a four-year veteran. The Warriors also threw in their first-round pick, the third one in the draft, so the Celtics chose Minnesota's Kevin McHale, a 6-foot, 10-inch forward. In the space of about 20 minutes, Auerbach had secured the best Celtics front court in their history.

These moves paid off immediately as Boston, with a rejuvenated Tiny Archibald running the offense, had a mid-season streak of 25 wins in 26 games, then hung on to win the division title with a 98-94 victory over the Philadelphia 76ers on the final day. Two weeks later, these teams met again for the conference title, and the Sixers soon had a 3-1 lead. But in the fifth game, Boston, behind 109-103 with 1:51 to play, scored eight straight points (the last

two on Carr's foul shots), and won the game 111-109, with Parish intercepting a last-gasp Philly pass to seal the victory. Philadelphia was coasting along in the sixth game until some of their fans at the Spectrum abused Maxwell when he flew into the stands to retrieve a loose ball. A melee ensued and lit a fire under the stodgy Celtics, who came from 17 points down to win 100-98, capped by McHale's steal on Andrew Toney as he tried for a last-second, tie-making shot.

The seventh game was in Boston, and again it was the Celtics' defense that helped rally the team from an 89-82 deficit by holding the 76ers without a field goal for the last five minutes of the game, en route to a 91-90 win. Bird, who had battled Julius Erving and Bobby Jones toe-to-toe throughout the series, made one of his greatest plays when he took the ball the length of the court, pulled up about 23 feet from the basket and canned a jump shot for a 91-89 lead with 93 seconds to play. A few seconds later, with Maurice Cheeks about to shoot two fouls for Philadelphia, Carr walked past, patted him on the butt and whispered, "Don't choke." Cheeks missed one of the shots and Boston rode out the game without another threat.

After that heart-stopping series, the Celts got into a 2-2 tie against the Houston Rockets for the NBA title before Moses Malone taunted Maxwell, who exploded with a 28-point, 15-rebound performance in a 109-80 fifth game victory. It was easy after that as the Celtics rolled to a 17-point lead in the fourth quarter of the deciding game, and Bird scored seven points in the final two minutes for a 102-91 victory and the team's 14th NBA title.

Philly and Boston battled each other for a third straight conference title the following season, and again the Celts, handicapped when Archibald separated his shoulder in the second game, fell behind 3-1. "Well, one thing we know for certain is that it can be done, because we did it," Chris Ford noted. And they almost did it again. The Celtics battled back with an 88-75 win to tie the series, the tie-maker reminiscent of other previous victories in the Spectrum.

Basketball historians and Celtics fans alike were unanimous in their belief that the Celtics would again do the impossible, because the seventh game was at Boston Garden, where no Philadelphia team – Warriors or 76ers – had ever won a seventh game. But try as they might, Boston never caught the magic of years past that afternoon, and Philadelphia cruised to a 120-106 victory.

That started the downhill part of the Coach Fitch era, as the following season the Celtics again made the playoffs, but were blown away in four straight games by the Milwaukee Bucks. The team was mentally spent, worn out by Fitch's intense coaching style and tremendous work ethic. The coach's absolute mania for preparation, even to watching videotapes of an opponent in the locker room shortly before a game, seemed to undermine his players' natural enthusiasm and rhythm. Some people thought Fitch's style derived from his discomfort with Auerbach or even with the championship banners that hung from the Garden's rafters. They represented another era to him, and he wanted to divorce himself from the Celtics' past and build his own era, never understanding the real secret of the franchise's success is the Celtics Pride that forever interweaves the past with the present.

Below: *The end and the beginning of two Celtics eras: Dave Cowens (18, first row) with the 1980 team in his final season and Larry Bird (33, back row) in his first season with Boston.*

9. Soaring Through the Eighties

K. C. Jones had sat very quietly on one end of the Celtics' bench during the coaching regimes of Tom Sanders, Dave Cowens and Bill Fitch, largely unappreciated by many around him except for those players who understood that his depth of knowledge, experience and understanding of the game was in no way related to his quiet manner. That is why there were smiles all around when Red Auerbach named his old player, who had taken the Washington Bullets to the NBA finals in 1975, to succeed Fitch as head coach. When the 1984 season ended, no one smiled broader than Auerbach as K. C. steered the Celtics to their 15th NBA championship.

K. C. was a precise opposite to Fitch. He allowed the players to be themselves on the court, to become creative within his style of offense, and to blend their talents and personalities into his game plans. He accepted their input as long as it worked within the overall scheme, and his cool, quiet manner seemed a blessed relief from the intense Fitch. As a result, the Celtics relaxed and allowed their considerable talents, with the guiding hand of Jones gently steering them in the right direction, to take over.

The Celtics were a much different team than the one that had won the 1981 title, thanks largely to the maturing of Kevin McHale, and the addition of guards Danny Ainge and Dennis Johnson and center Bill Walton. Jones had a team of great depth, with such subs as forward Scott Wedman and guards Jerry Sichting and Gerald Henderson, as well as Walton and Greg Kite at center or forward.

McHale had become a dominant force

Above: *Bill Fitch was head coach of the Celtics from 1979-83 and won the 1981 NBA title. His relentless routines wore out the team.*

Right: *Kevin McHale, a first round draft pick from Minnesota in 1980, was nearly impossible to stop with his great arm reach and array of moves near the basket.*

from the first moment he joined the team, when he was the first rookie "sixth man" since John Havlicek. He was magnificent in this role as he spelled both Cedric Maxwell and Larry Bird, until becoming a starter after Maxwell was dealt to the Los Angeles Clippers in 1985. Some claim he is the best scoring forward in NBA history, and that is tough to refute because it is almost impossible to stifle his deadly turnaround jump shot, his variety of hook shots, and his endless variety of fakes and moves close to the basket. On defense, his long arms helped to make him a voracious shot-blocker and rebounder.

Danny Ainge once noted that both Kevin McHale and Larry Bird were so confident of their ability to score that when they were posted against a defensive player, they often taunted him, daring him to stop them. In the 1985 season, McHale set a club scoring record of 56 points one afternoon against Detroit, and Bird kidded him afterward, telling him he should have made it 60 points because it might last longer. A week later, Bird broke it with 60 points.

Auerbach strengthened the club defensively by trading reserve center Rick Robey to Phoenix for guard Dennis Johnson, who had been the MVP of the 1979 NBA playoffs when he was with Seattle. Johnson had a reputation for being moody and selfish, but once he landed in Boston, he became the consummate team player and eagerly adapted to his new role as playmaking guard. But that was only half the equation, because the Celtics also coveted his defensive skills. Boston had not been able to cope with a big, strong, mobile guard like Andrew Toney of Philadelphia, and knowing the 76ers were apt to be their roadblock to future NBA titles, they correctly believed DJ could shut him down. He did all of that and more, and Bird later called him "the best player I ever played with."

Johnson soon was joined by Ainge in the back court, after the Celtics first convinced the former Brigham Young University All-America to forego a major league baseball career with the Toronto Blue Jays, and then paid that team a reported $800,000 as compensation before handing Ainge a million dollar-plus contract. It was a worthy investment because the fiery Ainge was a healthy contrast to the cool efficiency of the four other starters. He dove for balls and charged wildly through defenses in the same style as that of his boyhood idol, Pete Maravich, who had ended his own NBA career just a few years earlier in Boston. This ribald style soon made him the darling of Boston Garden, while in other NBA cities, he became the Celtics player everyone loved to hate.

Above left: *The Celtics obtained guard Dennis Johnson from Phoenix to add defense and leadership to their backcourt. He helped lead them to a pair of NBA titles and four trips to the NBA finals.*

Above: *Guard Danny Ainge gave up a major league baseball career with Toronto to play for Boston (1981-89). A fiery competitor and a fine three-point shooter, Ainge returned to the Celtics in 2003 as Executive Director of Basketball Operations.*

In the 1984 playoffs, the Celtics had to overcome a great one-man performance by Bernard King of the Knicks that helped carry that series to seven games, and when they played the Los Angeles Lakers for the title for the first time in 15 years, they needed more than just a bit of luck to win in seven games. This series also accentuated the Larry Bird–Magic Johnson rivalry as the NBA's two preeminent players. They had matched each other in the NCAA championship final in 1979, and Johnson's Michigan State Spartans had won over Bird's Indiana State team quite handily. Both then entered the NBA in the fall and ever since had been vying for dominance both on the court and in the marketplace, where products bearing their names and likenesses had become prolific.

Johnson and the Lakers had all but clinched a 2-0 series lead when Lakers rookie James Worthy tossed a lazy inbounds pass, and Gerald Henderson swooped in, scooped it up and raced to the basket to tie the game, for the biggest play of his six-season Celtics career. Scott Wedman's basket then won the second game in overtime. When the teams returned to Boston tied 2-2, old Boston Garden became another Celtics "sixth man" because the old barn, with no air conditioning, registered a sweltering 97 degrees for the fifth game. Bird, who had endured endless summers of blistering heat honing his considerable skills on the playgrounds in his native Indiana, hit 15 of 20 field goals to give Boston a 3-2 lead. The Lakers then won in Los Angeles, but Cedric Maxwell saddled up his teammates, telling them, "Jump on my back," and with help from Ainge coming off

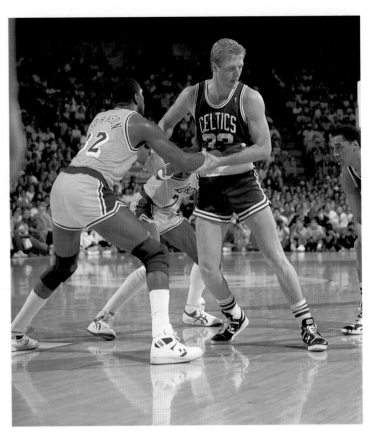

Above: *The Celtics defeated the Lakers for the NBA title in 1984 for the eighth time, and won the deciding seventh game against them for the fourth straight time.*

Above right: *The rivalry between Larry Bird and the Lakers' Magic Johnson made for some of the most inspired play in the NBA in the 1980s.*

the bench, he helped the team to a 111-102 title-clinching victory.

Two years later, the Celtics were back for another NBA title, having lost to the Lakers in the NBA finals for the first time ever in 1985 when, without Maxwell, Boston could not match the Lakers' firepower and rebounding, and went down in six games. In 1986 matters were entirely different, and many believe the key acquisition was Bill Walton, a gifted center who had been a three-year All-America with UCLA's national champions during the 1970s, and then had led Portland to the 1977 NBA title before being hampered by an endless series of foot injuries. Coming to Boston was his last hurrah, and he provided the Celtics with a deadly rotation in their front court that bedeviled opponents throughout the season. He provided much-needed relief for Parish at center, and also spelled McHale at strong forward. Walton not only was a great trigger for the Celtics' offense because of his superb passing and rebounding skills, but his last injury-free season also made him a consistent contributor.

The Celtics were deadly at home, winning all but one of their 41 games en route to a 67-15 record. Ironically, the turnaround point of the season came on Christmas Day in New York, when the team blew a 25-point lead against the hapless Knicks and lost the game in double-overtime. Embarrassed as well as enraged, they ripped off 17 wins in the next 18 games and rolled through the season, thanks in part to the depth from a "White Team" and a

"Green Team," denoted by the color of the jerseys they wore in practice. The White Team included the nominal starters, the Green Team the subs who scrimmaged against them every day. The Green gang, including Walton, Wedman and Sichting, became the shock troops, coming into a game while the varsity was resting on the bench and blitzing the opposition to make the job easier for the starters when they returned.

All of this got them into the finals against Houston for the second time in the decade, and as in the earlier joust, the Celtics won, securing their 16th NBA championship in six games. The highlight of the series may have been a David vs. Goliath battle that featured Boston's "little" 6-foot, 1-inch guard Sichting against Houston's 7-foot center Ralph Sampson. Celtics fans retain the lasting image of Walton celebrating with his teammates as the final seconds of the clinching game wound down. The great veteran reveled in his final shining moment that being a part of the Celtic legend had made possible.

The Walton magic ended the following season when his foot injuries recurred and he saw little action, causing an outage in the Celtics' front court power rotation which was felt most of all during the finals against the Lakers, who won the series in six games. This seemed to trigger the disappearance of all of the good fortune that had belonged to the Celtics, and in its place came tragedy and serious injury. First came the death of top draft pick Len Bias only a few hours after his draft selection in 1987. Then McHale broke his foot but played on it through a losing playoff series against the Detroit Pistons, while Bird endured a continual rash of back injuries, and Parish – without the once formidable Walton to relieve him – had to play with elbow, leg and ankle miseries that hampered him.

Still it was a grand run for most of the 1980s, and brought a whole new pantheon of heroes to Boston, giving a fresh generation of fans a cast that stood on a par with those from the glorious Bill Russell and Dave Cowens eras.

Left: *Bill Walton had one last NBA hurrah with the Celtics in the 1986-87 seasons, helping them defeat Houston for the 1986 championship. But foot miseries hampered him during the 1987 season and in the NBA championships, where the Celtics lost for the first time in the finals against the Lakers.*

10. Welcome to the Nineties

Below: *Reggie Lewis played college basketball at Northeastern University, only a couple of miles from Boston Garden. The Celtics' top draft pick in 1987, he died tragically of a heart attack in 1993.*

There is nothing like a new decade to freshen up the Celtics and get them energized for another dose of success. Consider that Red Auerbach joined the team in 1950 and worked his magic; Tom Heinsohn's first season was 1970; and Bill Fitch started revitalizing the Celtics in the 1980 season. So it was that a few weeks after the

conclusion of the 1990 season, Chris Ford became head coach. Auerbach also turned over the day-to-day basketball operations to Dave Gavitt, former commissioner of the Big East Conference and once a very successful college basketball coach. Of course, Red kept his hand in the club's operation to whatever degree he believed necessary.

Ford replaced Jimmy Rodgers after having stoically endured a needless coaching search by Gavitt outside the organization. Ford had played for the Celtics for the final five years of his 12-season NBA career, and had been an assistant coach for seven seasons under both Jones, who had moved to the front office after the 1988 season, and Rodgers.

Rodgers was released at the end of the 1990 season following a humiliating loss to the Knicks in the playoffs when Boston blew a 2-0 lead. Rodgers, who came to the Celtics as an assistant coach to Fitch and stayed in the same post under Jones, once had been so highly regarded as a future head coach by Auerbach that he refused permission for the Knicks to interview him. Instead, Auerbach moved Jones to the front office, and gave Rodgers the job in the 1989 season. Rodgers set out to spruce up an aging team, and looked on track as Reggie Lewis, a homegrown collegian from Northeastern University, emerged as a future star when he picked up much of the slack after Larry Bird missed most of the year with foot injuries. Top draft pick Brian Shaw brought enough quickness and verve to the back court that the Celtics traded Danny Ainge, and his good three-point shooting ability, to the Sacramento Kings for front-courtmen Ed Pinckney and Joe Kleine so that McHale and Parish would get some relief.

This wasn't enough, as Boston was eliminated in the first round of the playoffs, and the rebuilding scheme derailed a bit in 1990 when Shaw left to play in Italy for a million dollars; Lewis had to learn a new job in the back court; and Bird took an entire season to work himself back into game shape. Yet, many believe that Rodgers' inability to demand more of his players during periods

Left: *Larry Bird was hampered by back problems during the latter half of the 1991 season and throughout the playoffs but still was the key weapon that helped Boston to its first Atlantic Division title since 1988. Bird retired at the end of the 1991-92 season.*

Above: *Guard Dee Brown, the Celtics' number one draft pick in 1990, brought speed and aggression to the backcourt.*

Opposite: *Well-versed in the ways of Celtics Pride, Chris Ford played for (1978-82) and coached (1990-95) the team.*

the court. The Celtics responded in grand style, winning 29 of their first 34 games in the 1991 season, and took the Atlantic Division title.

There were several keys to this high intensity level of play:

• Robert Parish, though the oldest player in the NBA at age 36, had the best overall season of his career.

• Larry Bird was fully recovered from his problems for the first half of the year, and this offensive style was perfect for his on-court direction and ability to hit open men on the move.

• Kevin McHale came off the bench as "sixth man," with Kevin Gamble starting at forward. Gamble was more effective on the move, and McHale supplied big bursts of offense against players unable to cope with his skills.

• Brian Shaw returned from his one-year Italian hiatus and picked up the tempo. His return was forced by a federal court in Boston that ruled a contract he signed with the Celtics while playing in Italy was valid and that he had to honor it.

• Reggie Lewis matured into a confident and productive NBA back-court player, adding scoring and stability.

• Rookie number 1 pick Dee Brown brought speed, rebounding and aggressive play to his stint as number three guard, and before the season had ended, he had improved to such a degree that he and Shaw were splitting time in the back court.

But during the second half of the season, the old injury bugaboo caught up with the Celtics and hampered them right into the playoffs. Bird was all but crippled by his chronic back problems, forcing him even to lay on the floor by the Celtics' bench when he was not in the game. He missed several games near the end of the season and rarely practiced, badly hampering his scoring. McHale sprained his ankle in February and never was fully mobile for the remainder of the season.

All of this affected them in the playoffs, where they struggled to get past Indiana in the first round – the first time since 1988 they had advanced past that point. They took a 2-1 lead against the defending NBA champion Detroit Pistons, but then lost the next three, though they came from 18-point deficits in the fourth quarter of the last two games before losing. In the final game, Parish was sidelined with a pair of sprained ankles, Bird was rendered nearly useless by his injuries, and the Celtics finally lost in overtime.

But no one hung his head. They had played in the Celtics tradition, with a lot of heart. That, and the promise of the future, was enough – that was always enough.

of erratic play, and his over-control during games, choked off the team and finally brought his downfall in the Knicks' playoff series, causing Auerbach to begin a new era with Chris Ford.

The new coach not only knew the strengths and weaknesses of the players, but most importantly he understood the philosophy by which the Celtics organization was directed. Ford restored the running game and uptempo offense that always had been part of the Celtics' style, and he allowed the players more latitude on

11. Lost in the NBA's Wilderness

The third great era of Celtics domination crashed for good in the early 1990s. The Big Three of Bird, Parish and McHale was finished, physically wrung out after more than a decade of providing Boston with the same excellence that had made the Celtics the NBA's preeminent franchise since the Bill Russell era began in 1956.

The loss of those three players, as well as their great supporting cast that included guards Danny Ainge and Dennis Johnson, was not unexpected given their years of NBA service and their ages. But what was unexpected was that their departure would mire the team in relative mediocrity for most of the next 15 years.

It really wasn't until deep into the 2008 season that Celtics' followers dared to talk about a potential NBA championship while the team was en route to producing the NBA's best win-loss record that

season. When the Bird era, the team's third dynasty, had finally ended in the early nineties, that kind of talk was commonplace. After all, hadn't the Celtics survived the retirements of such superstars as Bill Russell, Bob Cousy, Dave Cowens, John Havlicek & Co. while winning 16 world championships?

And couldn't majordomo Red Auerbach revert to his role as presiding genius and orchestrate another rebuilding program to restore the team to its traditional championship status? In hindsight, it seemed that everyone—the Celtics organization and fans alike—became victims of a mass attack of wishful thinking that new dynasties could be created with a snap of Auerbach's fingers.

First, some historical background behind that illusion. In 1957, the Celtics' first dynasty was formed when Russell and a

Below: *Robert Parish, Kevin McHale, and Larry Bird, three stars of the Celtics' glory years, are here pictured at Larry Bird Night at Boston Garden on February 4, 1993, a tribute to Bird after he had retired in 1992.*

tough, hard-nosed rookie forward from Holy Cross named Tom Heinsohn finally complemented the backcourt skills of Bob Cousy and Bill Sharman. That dynasty, which added other key parts as it moved along, had produced 11 NBA titles in 13 years by the time Russell & Co. had finished their careers. As previously noted, at the end of the 1969 season after the 11th championship banner was assured, it seemed almost incongruous to Celtics followers that arguably the greatest player in NBA history was no longer a Celtic.

But the fans' disillusionment lasted only for the 1970 season before the next dynasty was formed by players carried over from the Russell era such as John Havlicek, Don Chaney and Don Nelson. This core was joined by Dave Cowens, Paul Silas, Jo-Jo White and Charlie Scott, producing seven consecutive winning seasons, including a pair of NBA titles. That seventies dynasty, without the overpowering talent of a superstar like Russell (and later the Bird-McHale-Parish triumvirate), had mostly disappeared in the 1978 and 1979 seasons. There was a feeling of general satisfaction that the team had gotten all it could from the talent on hand, but also a feeling of optimism that another such dynasty was already on Auerbach's drawing board.

Sure enough, in the 1978 draft, Auerbach chose then-Indiana State University junior Larry Bird as a future number one pick—and the third Celtics dynasty was born. Bird joined the remnants of Cowens' last great team in 1979. A year later, with the help of newcomers Robert Parish and rookies Kevin McHale and Danny Ainge, plus such holdovers as Cedric Maxwell, Chris Ford, Nate Archibald and Rick Robey, the Celtics won the 1981 title. During the eighties, Auerbach put together Celtics teams that produced five NBA title runs with three world championships before time and injury began to take a toll on the Big Three of Bird, McHale and Parish in the early nineties.

Auerbach took a huge step in the late eighties to try to continue the Celtics' championship runs when he drafted Maryland all-America forward Len Bias in 1987 and Northeastern University forward Reggie Lewis two years later. Bias and Lewis were seen as not only becoming prime parts of that championship team, but as key players who would become the bridge leading to an eventual fourth dynasty.

But the fates that had been so kind in the three previous rebuilding programs finally turned their backs on the Celtics when the franchise suffered two disastrous

Above: *Danny Ainge, Celtics standout player (1981-89) and since 2003 Executive Director of Operations for the team, here blocks "Doc" Rivers of the Atlanta Hawks in a 1988 game. Rivers became the Celtics' coach in 2004.*

Above left: *Dominique Wilkins, a Celtics nemesis during most of his career, came to Boston for his final three NBA seasons (1992-95). Although he got the best of Chicago's Scottie Pippen in this 125-109 Celtics victory in a 1994 game, he arrived too late to break a championship drought.*

Above right: *Sherman Douglas, here driving in for a layup against the Sacramento Kings, was the only bright spot in the Celtics' 1994 season when he finished second among the NBA's assists leaders with 8.8 per game.*

and crushing losses. First, Bias died from an overdose of drugs just hours after the Celtics had drafted him. He was projected to be part of an almost unbeatable rotation with Bird and McHale at forward, with the plan of Bias stepping in as a full-time player when Bird's career was finished. Bird had already begun to show signs that his body was breaking down and could not sustain the game-to-game pounding.

Lewis, who had already proven himself the perfect fit by shifting to guard from his college position of forward, was a critical contributor to the team before he was stricken with a fatal heart attack after the 1993 season. The projected "Dynasty Four" had crashed and burned before it ever got off the ground.

The timing could not have been worse as the careers of Bird, McHale and Parish all ended around the same time. By 1992, Bird's chronic back problems had made him barely a part-time player during the season and as

a member of America's "Dream Team" in the Olympic Games in Barcelona, Spain. He retired before the start of the 1993 season, but instead of having Bias ready to pick up the load, the Celtics had no one to replace their greatest all-around player. He left as the team's all-time leader in points per game (24.3) and free throw accuracy (3,960 of 4,471 for 88.6%); second all-time in scoring (21,791), field goals attempted (17,334) and made (8,591); third in assists (5,695); fourth in minutes played (34,443), foul tries made (3,960) and rebounds (8,974); fifth in three-point field goal accuracy (649 of 1,727 for 37.6%); and seventh in games played (897), field goal accuracy (8,591 of 17,334 for 49.6%) and free throw attempts (4,471).

Within two more seasons, Parish and McHale also were gone. Parish ranks second in Celtics history in games (1,106) and rebounds (11,051); third in minutes played (34,977), total points (18,245), field goals (7,483), and field goal accuracy (7,483 of 13,558 for 55.2%); fifth in field goal attempts (13,558); and sixth in free throws attempted (4,491) and made (3,279).

McHale, almost unstoppable around the basket with his height and long arms, retired for the Celtics second in field goals made (6,830 of 12,334 for 55.4%); third in games (971); fourth in total points (17,335) and made field goals (6,830); fifth in free throws attempted (4,554) and made (3,634); sixth in rebounds (7,122), minutes played (30,118); and eighth in field goal attempts (12,334).

The Celtics and their followers had been spoiled by a quarter century of near constant success. It was almost taken for granted that those halcyon days would continue unabated, the losses of Bias and Lewis not withstanding. There were some key replacement parts seemingly set in the early nineties with guards Brian Shaw and Dee Brown, bringing hopes among the Celtics faithful that other nuggets were waiting to be unearthed from elsewhere in the NBA by Auerbach's shrewd wheeling and dealing.

But it was not to be this time. The result was the 15-year drought that reached into the first decade of the new millennium. The reasons were varied. Unlike past years, the Celtics could never sign a star of the Bird-McHale-Parish caliber until they drafted Paul Pierce in 1998. The internal change that took place within the organization also found Auerbach being pushed into the background as a chief operating officer in favor of new executives such as Dave Gavitt and later Rick Pitino.

Auerbach was one-of-a-kind and those who succeeded him paled in comparison with his all-around ability to judge playing talent; nor did they possess his shrewdness or the skills needed to acquire future Hall of Famers. Furthermore, newer executives in the NBA, having watched Auerbach pull off deals that produced Bird, McHale and Parish (the latter two were part of one trade with Golden State that was truly an Auerbachean masterpiece), shied away from dealing with him.

A salary cap within the NBA also had been instituted making player movement much freer and driven by money, which benefited the teams owned by a new generation of young millionaires who spent lavishly to acquire talent. Player drafts had no limitations so that there were no caps on eligibility. Players often came to the pros right out of high school and few college stars ever accumulated a full four years of experience. As a result, they were often less equipped to handle the game.

There were a few good moments contained in the Celtics' infrequent playoff appearances. But for a team with such a rich history of star-studded talent, there was now only Pierce, a first-round draft pick from Kansas, who could be put in the "superstar" category. But even superstars need superior players to be successful and the Celtics did not attract enough who could complement Pierce's great talent until the 2008 season when they obtained Kevin Garnett and Ray Allen in trades.

The reality of this talent dearth really didn't sink in with Celtics followers in the nineties. It was during those dark years that coach Rick Pitino once was moved,

Above: *Antoine Walker, a first round draft pick in 1996, became the first Celtics player to make the NBA All-Star team since 1992. He led the team in scoring in 1994 with a 22.4 average. He and Paul Pierce were the best Celtics duo in a decade.*

Left: *Rick Fox shoots against the Sacramento Kings during a game at the Boston Garden on October 26, 1993.*

Above: *Coach Rick Pitino, here with Ron Mercer, had less success in the NBA than in college basketball, where he has achieved great success before and after his stint as head coach with the Knicks and the Celtics.*

Right: *Dino Radja, a native of Croatia, was the first foreign-born player to star for the Celtics. Only the sixth Celtics rookie to amass 1,000 points in a season, he also made the NBA's All-Rookie team.*

to miss 26 games and posting a career low in scoring (780 points). Further, the greatest power forward in the team's history found his effectiveness around the basket severely limited, grabbing only 330 rebounds during his limited playing time.

While Parish was beginning to show his 39 years, he still scored 1,115 points. The team was saved by the great all-around play of Reggie Lewis, who scored 1,707 points and established himself as a bona fide NBA star in just his fifth NBA season. But the team was eliminated in the second round of the playoffs.

In the 1993 season, the Celtics had added forward Xavier McDaniel to replace Bird but dropped eight of their first 10 games and 12 of their first 29. Still, the team had enough left to post a 36-17 record in the second half of the season and make the playoffs with an overall 48-34 record. Few realized it at the time, but returning to that old comfortable spot in post-season play was to become a rarity for most of the next 14 seasons.

The 1993 playoff series against Charlotte, the second of four recent NBA expansion teams to make the playoffs, was a disaster. Not only were the Celtics eliminated in four games, but in the series opener Lewis collapsed on the court. He was later diagnosed with arrhythmia, or irregular heartbeat. It was the first sign of a condition that killed Lewis three months later on July 27, 1993, while he was shooting baskets alone at the Celtics practice facility at Brandeis University outside Boston. He was found by paramedics in complete cardiac arrest and died shortly thereafter. Lewis' tragic and untimely death marked the end of Auerbach's grand design to build yet another dynasty.

In 1993-94, there was no way in which the Celtics could survive both the loss of Lewis and the retirement of McHale after the 1993 season. They compiled their worst season (32-50) since 1979, the year before Bird arrived. The only bright spot was the emergence of rookie Dino Radja, a 6-11 forward from Croatia whose national teams were becoming fertile recruiting territory for the NBA. Radja ranked second on the team in scoring behind guard Dee Brown with 15.1 points per game (Brown had 15.5 points per game) and earned a spot of the NBA all-Rookie second team. He also was the sixth rookie in Celtics history to amass more than 1,000 points in a season, joining Cousy, Heinsohn, Havlicek, Cowens and Bird. The only other bright spot that year was guard Sherman Douglas who finished second among the NBA's assists leaders with 8.8 per game.

in a fit of frustration, to forcibly point out that "Larry Bird, Kevin McHale and Robert Parish will not be coming through those doors." Pitino was trying to drive home the point that the glory days of that third Celtics dynasty were long gone and everyone needed to get over it.

Perhaps fans were slow to realize the depth of the problem because at first the descent was masked by two passable back-to-back seasons in 1992 (Bird's final season) and 1993, both of which ended with brief playoff appearances. Bird was barely operating in 1992 and his sparse (for him) 908-point total foretold his decision to retire before the 1993 season. McHale's bad ankles caused him

At the end of the 1994 season, the Bird dynasty officially ended when Parish left the team to sign with Charlotte as a free agent. In a move aimed at revitalizing the sagging franchise, M.L. Carr, the peppy defensive specialist from the team's 1990s title teams, was made general manager, further pushing Auerbach away from any heavy day-by-day involvement and leaving the personnel decision-making to others. Carr brought free agents Dominique Wilkins and Pervis Ellison to Boston for the 1994-95 season. Though both players were past their primes, they still had enough left to help the Celtics slip into the final playoff spot with a very un-Celtics-like 35-47 record under coach Chris Ford.

The Celtics started the 1996 season with Carr as the head coach and, after abandoning the famed Boston Garden, moved literally six inches to a new facility (that was the space between the two buildings) that some still call the "Garden," but whose official name has undergone several name changes, depending upon its corporate ownership. Of course, the Celtics retained their trademark parquet floor in the new building. But with such a spotty home record since leaving the old Garden, some wondered whether the Celtics' good luck leprechaun had made the move with them, or had found another home.

Much of that spotty record had to do with team management, particularly the continued transition of players and coaches. Five head coaches—Auerbach, Russell, Heinsohn, Bill Fitch and K.C. Jones—had produced 16 world championships over three decades; during the next two decades, from 1988 through 2007, seven coaches—Jimmy Rodgers, Ford, Carr, Pitino, Jim O'Brien, John Carroll and Glenn (Doc) Rivers—had tried but failed to hang a 17th championship banner in the rafters of the new building. It is a coaching maxim that this veritable merry-go-round of leadership with its varied philosophies and constant flow of players, precludes the stability that is so vital in producing a championship team, let alone one of dynastic proportions.

In 1996, the team suffered its third straight losing season—the first time that had happened since the 1946-50 span. Contrary to what has been dubbed as Celtics Pride, success was found in individual—not team—achievement. For instance, guard Dana Barros set an NBA record when he sank a three-point field goal in 89 consecutive games before the Knicks stopped him on January 12, 1996. In 1997, the Celtics' 50th season, the team suffered their worst season ever with a horrible 15-67 record. Part of the blame

can be pinned on a record 471 games that players missed because of injury.

But there also were a couple of positive developments, namely the acquisitions of Paul Pierce and Antoine Walker, that also happened during this time. Pierce was like a gift from heaven to the Celtics in the 1998 draft because no one expected that the junior from Kansas would last until the 10th pick of the first round. He quickly produced a boffo rookie season with 16.5 points, 6.4 rebounds and 1.71 steals per game. He was the NBA's Rookie of the Month in February 1999, and made the league's all-rookie team at the end of that season.

Those early feats were just previews of the career that Pierce has logged for the Celtics. His talents in an earlier era would have easily placed him among the elite in Celtics history—and he may well land there by the time his career is finished. But Pierce's feats came at a time when the team constantly struggled and did not dominate the NBA as teams and stars of the three earlier dynasties had done. There is no doubt that had Pierce played with any of the Russell-Cowens-Bird teams, he would have been one of their brightest stars, and his name would be spoken in the same reverential tones reserved for players of those eras.

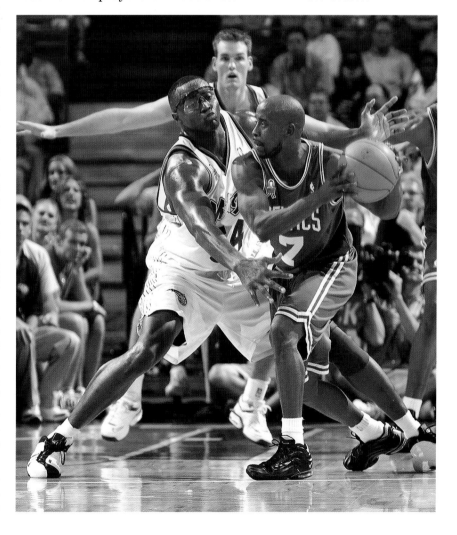

Below: *Guard Kenny Anderson, here battling Orlando's Horace Grant, came to the Celtics in 1998 from Toronto. He had more than 400 assists in two of his five seasons with the Celtics.*

Right: *Paul Pierce, who joined the Celtics in 1998, here attempts a lay-up against Lamar Odom of the Rookies in the 2000 Rookie All-Star Game.*

Far right: *Jim O'Brien succeeded Rick Pitino as head coach midway through the 2000 season. A .500 record over the remainder of the season earned him the job as head coach. The team made the playoffs each of his seasons, including 2004 when he resigned at mid-season.*

Pierce was always a star for the Celtics, regardless of the team's standing. He reached the 10,000-point mark faster than any Celtics player in history—431 games. It took Bird 436 games to achieve that mark and he played on much better teams. He also became the only player other than Bird to post four consecutive seasons with 3,000 or more minutes of playing time. He also matched Bird's record of scoring 2,000 or more points in four seasons. There is little doubt that when his playing days are finished, his No. 34 jersey will hang in the rafters of the "new Garden" with those of the greatest players who had been celebrated in the "old Garden."

Pierce joined Antoine Walker and Ron Mercer, both of whom had played for Pitino at Kentucky, to form a formidable trio in 1998. Until Walker was traded to Dallas before the 2004 season, his pairing with Pierce was the best front court duo the Celtics had since the Bird-McHale years. In Boston, Walker scored more than 1,000 points and averaged more than 20 points per game in six of his seven seasons as a full-time player (he had 391 when he returned for the last part of the 2004 season).

Walker was a first round draft choice in 1996 and responded with a 17.5 point scoring average, third among all NBA rookies. He became only the seventh Celtics rookie ever to surpass 1,000 points in a season. With Pitino as head coach in the 1998 season, Walker led the team in scoring and rebounding; his 22.4 point per game average was fifth in the NBA, and his 10.1 rebound average was seventh. He scored 40 points at Washington, tying the record for most points scored in one game by a Celtics player during the entire decade of the 90s. He also was the first Celtic player to participate in the All-Star Game since 1992.

During the 2000 season, the Pierce-Walker pairing finished 1-2 in seven of the team's regular season statistical categories. A year later, they combined to average 48.7 points per game, second only to the Lakers acclaimed duo of Shaquille O'Neal and Kobe Bryant (57.2). Pierce led the team with a 25.3 ppg average, just ahead of Walker's 23.4 mark. Pierce and guard Kenny Anderson, were the only two Celtics that season who played in all 82 games, and Pierce was the only player to log more than 3,000 (3,003) minutes. He also became the first Celtics player to surpass 2,000 points (2,071) since Bird scored 2,275 in the 1988 season. An indication of just how effective Pierce was working under the basket was his team record 738 free throw attempts that season. During the month of March 2001, he averaged over 30 points per game, 7.2 rebounds, 3.4

assists and 1.6 steals to earn NBA Player of the Month honors.

Walker starred in his own right that year. He led the NBA with a team record 212-of-603 three-point field goals, and was the league's only player to finish in the top twenty in points (23.4), rebounds (8.9), assists (5.5) and steals (1.7). Just for good measure, the Celtics captain led the team (third in the NBA) with 42 minutes per game.

Still, this production from the two Celtics' stars wasn't enough to save Pitino's job. After compiling a 12-22 record during the first third of the 2001 season, Pitino resigned as head coach and team president and was replaced in the coaching role by assistant Jim O'Brien. O'Brien carried the "interim" tag for the rest of that season, but after turning the team around to play on a .500 pace for the last 48 games, he became the team's 14th head coach at the conclusion of the 2001 season.

It was a good move because the Celtics finally produced some winning moments in 2002 as they embarked on a string of four consecutive playoff seasons—something not seen around Boston Garden since the heyday of the Bird era in the eighties. Part of the reason was a more disciplined style of play, ranking fifth in fewest turnovers with fewer than 14 per game.

The result was that O'Brien led the team to its first 40-victory season (49-33) since Chris Ford's 1992 team was 51-31. He also brought them to the playoffs for the first time since 1995, making it to the Eastern Conference finals before losing to New Jersey. A 22-19 road record was the team's best since the 1990 season.

Pierce and Walker, who once again made the NBA's 2002 Eastern Conference All-Star team, were key to the Celtics success. But they got a huge boost from a mid-season trade with Phoenix in which Boston received Rodney Rogers and Tony Delk in exchange for three players and a conditional 2002 first round draft pick.

Pierce had a fabulous season in 2002, becoming the first Celtics player ever to lead the NBA in scoring when he tallied 2,144 points while playing in all 82 games. He also became the first Celtic since Bird to exceed 2,000 points in back-to-back seasons as he quietly pursued Bird's team record four consecutive 2,000-point seasons that Larry had achieved in 1985-88. Pierce logged three in a row from 2001-2003, but didn't get his fourth until he put up 2,116 points in 2006.

Walker played in 81 games—he missed one because of injury—and was one of just four NBA players in 2002 to average more than 20 points per game (22.1), exceed

seven rebounds (8.0) and five assists (5.0). He also led the NBA for the second consecutive season in three point field goals with 222.

Showing that the 2002 season was no fluke, the Pierce-Walker duo led Boston to its second straight 40-victory season in 2003, the first time in a decade that the Celtics had accomplished that feat. It was also the first time since late in the Bird era that the Celtics had made consecutive playoff appearances.

Once again, the Pierce-Walker duo led the way, combining for more than 47 percent of the Celtics scoring, or 46 points per game, while playing more than three quarters of every game. Walker's 3,235 minutes ranked fourth in the NBA and Pierce got his third 2,000-point season with 3,096. Both players were twice named the Eastern Conference Player of the Week, and at the end of the season both were members of the Eastern Conference All-Star team. Pierce also led the NBA with a record-setting 80.2 percent free throw performance (604-753).

Left: *Raef LaFrentz here battles Indiana during the team's victory over the Indiana Pacers in an Eastern Conference semifinal playoff game. He was one of several young Celtics who helped the team to its fourth straight playoff appearance in 2005.*

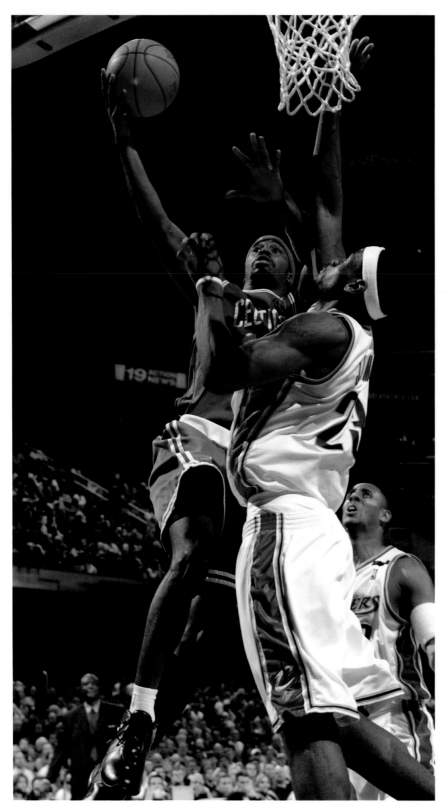

Above: *Ricky Davis scores on a lay-up over Cleveland's Labron James during a 2004 game in Cleveland. James became a formidable foe against the Celtics, both during the regular season and the playoffs.*

draft day when he traded draft rights in order to acquire guard Marcus Banks and standout high school center Kendrick Perkins. Then, halfway through the 2004 season, he changed coaches, replacing O'Brien with his assistant, John Carroll, and continued on the carousel by naming Glen (Doc) Rivers as head coach before the 2005 season.

Some claim that Ainge's seemingly frenetic effort to build a championship team had resulted instead in the Celtics being in constant flux—certainly not the way in which to build a consistent winner. Shortly before the 2004 season began, he shocked Celtics fans by trading Walker to the Dallas Mavericks in a five-player deal that also included a 2004 first round draft pick. Two months later, he pulled off a six-player deal with Cleveland that also included acquiring a second round draft pick. One of the players from that deal, veteran Ricky Davis, emerged later in the season as a perfect "sixth man," averaging 16 points per game with a 46 percent field goal average and hitting 34 percent from three-point range.

As noted previously, Pierce tied Bird's record with his fourth consecutive season of logging 3,000 or more minutes of playing time while also beating his pace to reach the 10,000 career points mark. All of this helped the Celtics back to their third consecutive playoff appearance, but they were eliminated in the first round by the Indiana Pacers.

Ainge's moves and Rivers' solid coaching job paid off in 2005 when the Celtics won the NBA's tough Atlantic Division title. It was the 29th time the team had won a division championship and the first time since 1992, before losing to Cleveland in Bird's final game as a Celtic. Although the team had acquired four players in the first round of the 2004 draft, only Tony Allen would stay with the team into the 2008 season. While the others made short-term contributions, the key deal was a late-season re-acquisition of Walker, then with Atlanta, in exchange for three players and a future first round draft pick. Walker's impact was immediate, helping the Celtics to a seven-game winning streak and a season-ending 18-9 run that led to the division title and a third straight match up against the Indiana Pacers in the playoffs. The seesaw series finally ended with Indiana winning the seventh game when the Celtics could only manage to shoot 37 percent from the field.

Walker again became expendable and was traded to Miami before the 2006 season, leaving Pierce to shoulder the leadership load as Ainge's youth policy loaded

The team defeated the Indiana Pacers in the first round of the 2003 NBA playoffs, but were eliminated for the second consecutive year by the New Jersey Nets.

The 2003 playoffs still were underway when the Celtics reached back into their rich history and named Danny Ainge, one of the stars of the Bird era teams, as Executive Director of Basketball Operations. One thing that marked Ainge's tenure in that post was his reluctance to stand pat. It seemed that bodies had been flying in and out of the Celtics locker room since he took over, beginning on his first more inexperience onto the Celtics roster. Too much inexperience, plus a spate of injuries, ended the team's playoff run, but never dimmed the luster of what was arguably the best season of Pierce's career. He became the first Boston player to score 30 or more points in 13 of 14 games during a mid-season run. He averaged a league-high 33.5 points per game during the entire month of February. Only Hall of Famer John Havlicek, in October 1970, had matched that feat. He also was one of just two players that season (Philadelphia's Allen Iverson was the other) to score at least 15 or more points in every game, helping him to achieve his fourth 2,000-point season to match Bird's team record. Pierce was the only NBA player that season to lead his team in points (26.8), rebounds (6.7), assists (4.7) and steals (1.4).

Pierce's absolute importance to the team was dramatically underscored by what happened when he didn't play during the 2007 season. He missed 42 games with an ankle injury and the team plunged to a miserable 24-58 record, its sixth worst record ever. Right in the middle of that terrible season was a record-setting 18-game losing streak, highlighting a period during which the team won just two of 27 games.

That was the culmination of a misery index in a year that began just a few days after Auerbach died at age 89. For several years beforehand, he had mostly confined himself to his home in Washington, D.C., where he had lived since his early coaching years at George Washington University before World War II. Few ever appreciated that Auerbach spent all of his seasons as Celtics head coach, and a great deal of his term as president and general manager, living out of a suitcase in a Boston hotel during the NBA season. But as his responsibilities waned and he became more of a caretaker and consultant than an active executive, his trips to Boston became more infrequent, and were further hampered by his fragile health. As noted earlier, he was hardly involved in the day-to-day operations of the team, but was always available as an adviser and also for his weekly luncheons with close friends in Washington at his favorite Chinese restaurant. A true legend of Celtics and NBA history had past.

The Celtics family received another jolt during the 2007 season when Dennis Johnson died suddenly while coaching a minor league team in California. The former all-pro guard was just 53 and it still is the avowed belief of those who knew him professionally and personally that he deserves to take his rightful place in basketball's Hall of Fame.

Pierce returned to play late in the 2007 season and the Celtics perked up, but not enough to escape the possibility that the team would be a prime candidate to land one of the two top picks in the draft lottery. Ainge's attempts at rebuilding the Celtics through the draft had not been very successful to that point because they had been unable to add a great complementary player or two to take the burden from Pierce.

The team suddenly found itself at a crossroads as to how its future would be determined. Looking for a proper direction, their eyes lit on the state of Minnesota to produce one of their greatest player acquisitions ever. Welcome to Boston, 12-year veteran and NBA All-Star, Kevin Garnett.

Below: *The bronze statue of "Red" Auerbach—with his ever-present cigar— is in Boston's Quincy Market, where, as these flowers attest, he remains a favorite of fans and tourists.*

12. Championship No. 17 The Birthright Returns

"It's time to go to work. We're ready."

So declared coach Doc Rivers after his Celtics polished off a victory over the New Jersey Nets in their final game of the 2008 season, punctuating a 66-16 record that topped the NBA during the 2007 season. In Celtics history, only the 1972 team (68-14) and the 1986 team (67-15) surpassed it. Interestingly, the latter was the last Celtics team to win an NBA championship until the 2008 team hung up the organization's 17th world championship banner.

In so doing, the Celtics achieved the biggest one-year turn-around in NBA history. They had finished the 2007 season with a dismal 24-58 record. Only a year later, the team turned in a record-setting swing of 42 victories that was attributed chiefly to the off-season acquisition of forward Kevin Garnett and guard Ray Allen, the coaching excellence of Glenn (Doc)

Rivers and an ownership that was totally dedicated to providing all the necessary resources to bring that to fruition.

Their season-long excellence began with winning 29 of their first 32 games. From that point on, there was little doubt that the team was ready to reclaim supremacy in the NBA, something that Celtics fans who rooted for the team from the mid-fifties through the mid-seventies considered a birthright.

There were a few bumpy spots during their 26 playoff games—an NBA record. But when the final seconds of the season had ticked away on June 17, 2008, the Celtics had won their first championship in 22 years—not since that 1986 team hoisted its championship banner into the rafters of the old Boston Garden in what became the exclamation point to the fabulous era of Larry Bird & Co.

Bird and his buddies were long gone when the 2008 series was played, but the

Below: *Dubbing themselves the "New Three," (L-R) Paul Pierce, Kevin Garnett and Ray Allen were unveiled before the start of the 2007-08 season as the heart of the revamped Boston Celtics.*

new Boston Garden (officially known as the TD Banknorth Garden) still smelled of the team's championship tradition with the dusty banners that hung from the arena's ceiling.

But as the team rolled up victory after victory during the 2007 season, players—present and past—pundits, and fans alike talked openly for the first time in a couple of decades of the possibility of the team again winning the NBA championship. Those feelings even spread to team legends such as Bill Russell, Bob Cousy, Tom Heinsohn, John Havlicek, Jo-Jo White and others who had helped to win those other 16 championship banners.

Those feelings even evoked the spirit of Celtics patriarch Red Auerbach, who had died in 2006 but had overseen as coach and/or general manager every single one of those previous NBA titles. Though only Rivers, a couple of his assistant coaches and team captain Paul Pierce had ever worked for him, Auerbach was proclaimed an inspirational force by the entire team, most of whom knew him only as a kind of mythical figure whose recreated signature was etched into their famed parquet basketball court.

All of Boston and their legion of fans across the country had marveled at the wonderful resurgence that had taken place in just one year. It was almost a storybook ending by a team that had won only those 24 games the previous season and was under fire from all directions because the organization had gone 22 years without a championship. That was two years longer than the Celtics had taken to win their first 16 NBA titles, making this success story all the more fantastic.

The answer to how this happened can be found in a sequence of events that began on the final day of 2002 when the team was purchased by a group of twenty Boston-area businessmen, led by Wyc Grousbeck, who were determined to endure whatever it took to rebuild the Celtics' proud heritage. During the next five years, the team made a couple of playoff runs but with meager results. Still, this ownership never flinched, despite spending millions of dollars in the face of ever-dwindling crowds and loyalty.

The owners' resolve was sorely tested after the horrible 2007 season when critics from all points were demanding a change in the team's basketball hierarchy, including Danny Ainge, the team's general manager and director of basketball operations, and Rivers as head coach. But instead of firing them, the ownership allowed Ainge to dismantle a team of potentially good, but still erratic, young players in favor of acquiring battle-hardened and talented veterans, particularly Minnesota's 6-11 Kevin Garnett, several-times an all-NBA forward. The result? Garnett helped to bring what Boston wanted immediately—an NBA title.

Above left: *The Alpha & the Omega of the Boston Celtics dynasty: Bill Russell (left), who led the Celtics to their first 11 NBA championships from 1957-69; and Kevin Garnett, who was so key in helping win the team's 17th title in 2008.*

Above right: *Celtics forward Kevin Garnett scores over former Minnesota Timberwolves teammate Corey Brewer (#22) during a 2008 pre-season victory at the O2 Arena in London.*

Above: *Gifted with the quickest hands on the Celtics, guard Rajon Rondo reaches in for one of his team-leading 129 steals in 2008 against the Washington Wizards' Gilbert Arenas.*

averaging just over ten points a game. Rondo also utilized hands as quick as a cobra strike when he led the team with 129 steals, saving his best performance of the season for the title-clinching sixth game of the Finals when he notched six steals to go along with 21 points, eight assists and seven rebounds.

Perkins, a 6-10, 265-pound giant, had come directly into the NBA from high school in 2003. He was originally drafted by Memphis, but was immediately traded to Boston. Now in only his second year as a starter, one of Perkins' greatest assets was his strength, which prevented opposing forwards and centers from muscling him out of position. During the NBA Finals, the Lakers' seven-foot, 260-pound center Pau Gasol gave up trying to play the muscle game against Perkins when he simply bounced off him. This forced Gasol to go elsewhere to try and find his shots and severely reduced his effectiveness.

Ainge also stocked his roster with effective veteran players James Posey, Eddie House and Scot Pollard before the 2007 season, and added Sam Cassell and P.J. Brown at mid-season. All of the wheeling and dealing put the Celtics $7 million over the NBA's luxury tax threshold of $68 million, forcing the team's owners to match that amount for surpassing the salary limit. But the ownership, having committed to Ainge and Rivers for their team's future, never batted an eye.

Those acquisitions gave the Celtics bench greater depth, talent and flexibility. For example, there was the 38-year old Cassell who had won two NBA championship rings with the Houston Rockets in the mid-90s as part of a career that brought him to eight NBA teams. He also had been a teammate of both Garnett at Minnesota and Allen at Milwaukee. The Celtics coveted Cassell because he also added 116 games of playoff experience in addition to giving Rondo the luxury of solid backup help. House also had won a championship ring, thus adding to the team's veteran backup support. Their presence particularly brought much-needed experience to a team that had very little post-season play. Added to that mix were nine-year veteran forwards James Posey, who also wore an NBA championship ring from Miami; holdover Leon Powe, a 6-8, 240-pound third-year veteran; and rookie Glen Davis, affectionately nicknamed "Big Baby." During the season, their presence made a huge difference in the Celtics' success. Powe, for example, was the key to five Celtics victories coming off the bench. When the team was finally assembled, it was an almost even split of returning

Added to that new mix was Milwaukee's all-pro guard Ray Allen, considered a cool, consistent point guard and deadly effective "pure shooter" during his 11 NBA seasons. Garnett and Allen became the primary components to revitalizing a team led by Pierce, a 10-year Celtics veteran who had labored valiantly with sub par teams but always played with a great standard of excellence.

While Pierce became the centerpiece of the new-look Celtics championship success in the 2008 season, two holdovers from the 2007 team helped immeasurably— Rajon Rondo and center Kendrick Perkins. Rondo was a second-year guard from Kentucky who had shown flashes of brilliance during his rookie season in 2007. As the 2008 season transpired, Rondo's potential increased to the point where he became a valuable contributor during the playoffs. Ainge and Rivers both believed Rondo would become a fine point guard and eventually run the Celtics offense, but they could not ignore his deft shooting touch and defensive and passing skills. He underwent a significant learning process under the crucible of a championship race,

veterans and new players. In making this transition, the Celtics went from being the NBA's second-youngest team in 2006-07 to becoming the league's fourth oldest in 2007-08.

But increased age seemed immaterial to the way the team pulled together in the 2007 season. This revitalized team helped Pierce, who had toiled in mostly unrecognized excellence with mediocre Celtics teams, achieve a long-sought break-out season. Some veteran Celtics watchers claim that Pierce is the most adept scorer in Celtics history, citing his proficiency to drive to the basket and score equally well with either hand. Others say that he is just as capable of drawing fouls and making free throws as he is making three-point shots; and still others claim that no Celtics player ever did so well in finishing off the fast break, which is quite a claim considering that the Celtics thrived on fast break offense for most of their championship years.

Since being joined by Garnett and Allen, Pierce also has played with a different attitude, scaling back his game to become part of a more balanced attack. True, he led the Celtics in scoring with 1,570 points and 19.6 points per game, but that was his lowest point total in eight seasons; and his 13.7 field goal attempts per game

were even fewer than he took during his rookie year. In the 2007 season, he added 411 rebounds, second to Garnett's team-leading total of 655. Pierce was so good that Garnett made him his personal choice for league MVP honors.

"He does a lot of things, just small little things that people don't see," Garnett said. "There are only three people I like to watch on offense and he's one of them. He makes scoring look easy. He has an uncanny confidence about him that I love, a cockiness and self-assuredness. He was one of the reasons I chose to come and play in Boston."

As usual, Pierce had his highlight reel moments during the 2007 season, sometimes on his own, but now often in tandem with Garnett and Allen. His season breakout game came in a 101-86 victory over Indiana. With ex-Celtics great Larry Bird, now the Pacers' president, looking on, he scored 31 points and grabbed 11 rebounds. Three days later against the Miami Heat, he hit the winning layup with 25 seconds to play for a 92-91 victory; and when the Celtics next played the Heat, Pierce scored 27 of the 33 points the Celts defense enabled by forcing Miami turnovers. When the Celtics played the Lakers in Los Angeles in their second of two 2007 season games, Pierce produced 33 points in a 110-91 victory.

Pierce really thrived working with the Garnett-Allen-Rondo combination and throughout the season one or more of them always seemed to pick up the team's offense and put it into a position to win the game. They were never better than during a 103-91

Above left: *Leon Powe makes a foul shot against the New York Knicks. Powe provided valuable depth to the Celtics frontcourt during their 2008 championship season.*

Above right: *Celtics fans considered Ray Allen (#20), Paul Pierce (#34) and Kevin Garnett (#5) to be a throwback to the trio of Larry Bird, Kevin McHale and Robert Parish who had led the Celtics to three NBA championships during the 80s.*

victory over Orlando in late December when Pierce led the team with 24 points followed by Rondo with 23, Allen scored 22 and Garnett tallied 21. In the first of two regular season games against the Lakers, Pierce had 20 points, six rebounds and nine assists to complement Garnett's 21 points and 11 rebounds, and Allen's 18 points, all of which led to a 107-94 victory.

It was a similar story for Garnett. Playing in his 13th NBA season after spending his entire NBA career as an all-star player with the Minnesota Timberwolves, Garnett became the eventual key to the Celtics' championship success because his presence set a superior leadership tone for the team, which was further enhanced by his great basketball skills. Rivers revised his offense to accommodate the increased firepower at his command, made even more powerful by Garnett's ability to dominate the middle of the floor with his size, and complement it with a deft shooting touch from the three-point range. Garnett was the team's second-leading scorer with 1,337 points, an 18.8 per game average, and was its top rebounder with 655, despite missing a nine-game stretch in the middle of the season because of injury.

Statistically, he delivered all that he promised. He registered 25 double-double games (double figures in scoring and rebounding), starting with the Celtics' opening game when he had 22 points and 20 rebounds in a 103-83 victory over Washington. A week later in a huge 106-83 win over Atlanta, he scored 27 points, grabbed 19 rebounds and added six assists and three blocked shots. When the Celtics defeated Houston on January 2, Garnett scored 11 of his 26 points in just seven minutes. Later that month he stole the ball in the final seconds to seal an 87-86 victory over Minnesota.

There is no way to quantify what Garnett's leadership accomplished. But one Celtics observer noted midway through the season, "The players seem to walk around with their heads up and with a new sense of pride in who they are. You can thank Garnett for that."

Allen was an 11-year veteran guard who had New England roots from his years playing for the University of Connecticut. His unflappable presence added to his

great offensive ability to produce firepower and leadership. In NBA parlance, Allen is known as a "pure shooter," particularly from three-point range—he led the team with 40 percent accuracy, making 180 of 452 shots from downtown. In all, Allen scored 1,273 points including 439 of 986 two-point field goals (44.5%) and a team-leading 90% of his foul throws.

"The benefits of that personnel turnover accrued during the season," noted ex-Celtics star Tom Heinsohn, "because Rivers was able to cease being what amounted to a high school coach in having to continually teach young players the fundamentals of playing in the NBA, and concentrate his talents on what he knew best—how to win in the NBA with players who already had learned those lesson." And Rivers was the ideal coach for a team whose veterans, at his insistence, showed the way for the younger players. His 13 seasons playing for Atlanta, the LA Clippers, New York Knicks and San Antonio prepared him for his first coaching stint with the Orlando Magic in 1999-2000. That team, much like his 2007 Celtics team, rose from the ashes and finished with a 41-41 record, earning Rivers honors as the NBA's Coach of the Year. He lasted four seasons at Orlando, then spent time as an analyst on ABC-TV's NBA Game of the Week before taking the Celtics job in 2004.

Like all good coaches, Rivers' style matches his personality. He is direct and clearly lays out what he expects of his players in everything they do that concerns Celtics basketball. Rivers disdains any labels but many have called him a "players coach" because he strives to maintain a positive relationship with all of his players, praising them when they excel, criticizing and correcting them when they don't. When he lays out a plan, he expects it to be followed—but, as Rivers showed when he tore down his young 2006-07 team and rebuilt it almost from scratch with veterans in 2007-08, he is not opposed to change.

Rivers knew that the key to making his revitalization plan achieve its ultimate goal—an NBA championship—depended on just how well the chemistry between this diverse group of players would work. Again, those close to the team give Garnett and Pierce much of the credit for maintaining a positive locker room morale; and give equal praise to Rivers for the manner in which he convinced the team to bend to his wishes. Reportedly there were times when there was strong but respectful debate among Pierce, Garnett and Rivers about the changes that were taking place. When Pierce finally bought into what Rivers was proposing, then it got done.

Rivers' biggest challenge in planning for the season was his insistence that the Celtics would be the best defensive team in the NBA. He continually stressed it with his team until it became a key part of their mindset throughout the season. "It's the old saw that while offense wins games, defense wins championships and that's what we're about," Rivers said. "The history of the great eras of this franchise occurred when it was dominant with its defense and we want to get back to those days."

Garnett's ability on defense was one of the main reasons why the Celtics went after him and he responded by leading the team with nearly ten rebounds a game. Perkins, the unmovable force at center, averaged six rebounds per game and Pierce chipped in with five. While Rondo led the team with 129 steals, Pierce and Garnett each surpassed 100.

Above: *Celtics coach Doc Rivers lays out his strategy for Paul Pierce (left) and Sam Cassell during the fifth game of the 2008 NBA Finals against the Lakers. Cassell was a valuable substitution at guard during the 2008 season.*

Above: *One of the great matchups during the Celtics-Cleveland Cavaliers series of the 2008 NBA Playoffs pitted the Cavs LeBron James (#23 with ball) against Kevin Garnett in the deciding seventh game. Though James was the game's top scorer with 45 points, Garnett had 13 rebounds and 13 points for Boston and sealed the 97-92 Boston victory with two free throws in the final eight seconds.*

Right: *Garnett (#5) leads a host of his Celtics teammates swarming after a rebound during Boston's 89-69 victory over the Sacramento Kings. The Celtics' renewed emphasis on defense led to their first win on the Kings' home court since 1986.*

But more than the obvious defensive statistics was the manner in which the Celtics *played* defense. Good defense really is a state of mind where the player must consciously determine to stop his opponent from scoring by physically working to shut him down, forcing him to turn the ball over or pass it to another teammate, or take away easy looks at the basket.

Rivers convinced his players that this emphasis on defense would be the Celtics' new style and they quickly dedicated themselves to the effort. Rivers had signed veteran coach Tom Thibodeau as his defensive aide. Thibodeau's imaginative and effective schemes throughout the season and the playoffs achieved all that Rivers intended. But it was not easy in the beginning because with players coming from a variety of teams, this meant not only scrapping previously learned defensive strategies and techniques but also changing individual attitudes. In reality, it was back to the total effort concept that was the hallmark of former great Celtics players such as Havlicek and Bird who led by example during their eras when they willingly crashed to the floor diving for loose balls. In this mode stood Pierce, still the team's centerpiece with the respect that he commanded from all the players, abetted by Rivers' ability to coax their acceptance. The results: Boston ranked first in field goal defense, allowing their opponents to make less than 42 percent of their shots. Their average of 42 rebounds per game was

12th in the NBA but they ranked second defensively by allowing opponents just 39.

On offense, the Garnett-Pierce-Allen trio averaged more than 55 points per game, and Rondo chipped in with ten more as his playing minutes increased. Pierce once again led the team with a 19.9 point average while Garnett, who missed nine games during a mid-season injury siege, finished with 18.8. Allen averaged 17.4 points.

When taken as a whole, all of those statistics produced a rollback to past generations when the Celtics ruled the NBA. At one point during the 2007 season, they had an astounding 41-9 record. They tied a team record by winning their first dozen road games; and two nights after setting that record, they recorded their ninth straight victory, tying the team's longest winning streak in 14 years.

Former "obstacles" started to crumble. The day after Christmas, they defeated the hometown Sacramento Kings for the first time in 11 years. Three days later, a 104-98 victory at Utah helped them surpass the 24-victory total of 2006-07; and 13 days after that, they tied the team record for the fastest pace to win their first 30 games. In a nine-day period early in March, the Celtics clinched a playoff berth with a 90-78 victory over Detroit;

defeated the Philadelphia 76ers 100-86 to achieve their first 50-win season since 1991-92; clinched the Atlantic Division title on March 14; and secured home court advantage throughout the playoffs on April 5 with a 101-78 victory at Charlotte, helped by winning streaks of seven, eight, nine (twice) and ten games.

All of this success led to a number of individual honors:

• Ainge was named 2007 Executive of the Year by *The Sporting News*.

• Garnett became the first Celtics player to be selected as Defensive Player of the Year (obviously this award did not exist during the Russell Era).

• Garnett also was named to his seventh NBA all-defensive first team, the first Celtics player to be honored since Kevin McHale in 1988, and the sixth Celtics player to make the team.

• Garnett and Pierce both made the all-NBA teams, Garnett as a first team selection for the fourth time; and Pierce was selected to the third team for the third time.

• An All-Star game starting berth for Garnett, and spots on the team for Pierce and Allen.

• Pierce was named MVP of the playoffs.

In the playoffs, though, Boston became a Jekyll and Hyde team. In their first two rounds against Atlanta and Cleveland, they won all of their home games and though they had the best road record in the NBA, they lost all of their road games. It took do-or-die seventh game victories at home to keep advancing. In the Eastern Conference championship series, their home winning streak was ended in the second game, but so was their losing streak on the road in their first game at Detroit. The Pistons tied the series 2-2 but Boston won the next two games, with the 94-75 clinching victory ironically coming on the road.

Finally, after 22 years of futility, the Celtics were back playing for an NBA title—and against the Los Angeles Lakers, their arch nemesis from the seventies.

Nostalgia ran wild. The series was tagged as a return to the glory days of the Lakers-Celtics rivalry in the eighties when the teams played each other in three NBA Finals and the Larry Bird-Magic Johnson rivalry was at it peak. The Lakers had defeated the Celtics 4-2 in 1987, the last time the teams met in a conference series and also the last time that Boston made it to the finals.

The 2008 NBA Finals, claimed the pundits, were to be a celebration of the flashy West Coast basketball style epitomized by the Lakers, and a reaffirmation that Kobe Bryant was indeed the greatest player on the planet. They disdained the first

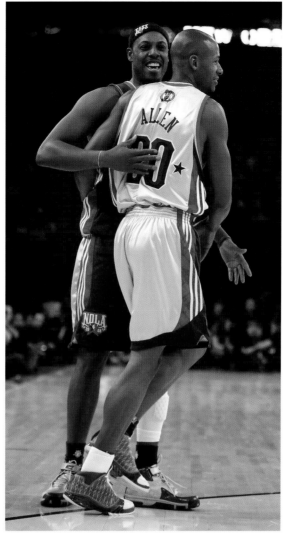

commandment of any playoff series that defense wins championships while totally overlooking the fact that the Celtics had the NBA's top defense.

Boston roared to a 2-0 series lead on their home floor, though they got a huge scare in the first game when Pierce was carried to the locker room after injuring his knee in a third quarter collision with Perkins. "I thought that was it," Pierce said after the

Left: *That All-Star Look: Celtics teammates Ray Allen (#20) and Paul Pierce share a laugh while providing a back-front look of their 2008 NBA All-Star Game uniforms. The duo played for the Eastern Conference team, which won the New Orleans thriller 134-128.*

Below: *A scary moment for Celtics fans: Paul Pierce holds his injured knee after a collision under the basket sent him toppling to the floor in the first game of the 2008 Finals against the Lakers. Luckily, Pierce quickly recovered and soon returned to the game.*

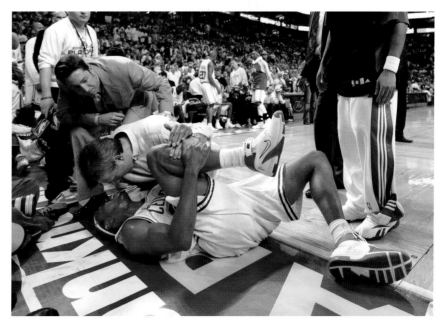

game. "I heard something pop and for a minute or so, I couldn't move the knee."

The crisis quickly passed and Pierce, welcomed back on the court with a huge ovation, immediately canned a couple of three-point shots as part of a 22-point performance.

The Celtics frittered away most of a 24-point lead in the fourth quarter of the second game, but Pierce saved them by making a flurry of free throws in the final seconds for a 108-102 victory. The win was largely fashioned by the improbable offense of Powe, who had played sparingly during the playoffs but came alive with 21 points. A gimpy Pierce, still hurting from his Game One collision, chipped in with 28 points and eight assists.

The Celtics squandered a good chance to go up 3-0 in the series when a spotty offensive performance—except for Ray Allen's 25 points—helped the Lakers to an 87-81 victory. Pierce missed 12 of 14 shots and scored a sorry six points while Garnett made just six of 21 shots for a measly 13 points.

The Lakers appeared to be back in synch in the fourth game and took a 24-point lead early in the second quarter. But the Celtics rose up in the third quarter with a 21-3 run and trailed just 73-71. The Lakers hung tough until there was 4:07 to play when a jump shot by Eddie House, one of the players that Ainge had signed early in the season to provide quick offense, gave Boston a lead it never relinquished to take a commanding 3-1 series lead.

All the talk about reliving Celtics-Lakers history then turned on the fact that no team had ever come from a 3-1 deficit to win an NBA title. And it didn't happen in 2008 either, though Bryant's 38-point performance helped the Lakers win the fifth game, 103-98. There were recriminations throughout the Celtics locker room afterward, particularly by Garnett who proclaimed that his 15-point, 13-rebound performance was "garbage." What hurt him most of all were two missed free throws with 2:31 to play that would have tied the game at 95.

That so-so effort along with the roaring crowd that greeted the Celtics at Boston Garden spurred Garnett to a dominating performance with 26 points and 14 rebounds in Game Six. The team knew that the packed arena wouldn't permit them to lose and the crowd's fervor expunged any possibility the team would sleepwalk through another game. Unlike the two previous games, Boston stayed with the Lakers from the start and built a gradual lead until their 15-2 explosion ending the first half gave them a commanding 58-35 advantage.

The second half featured the Celtics at their best. Allen, who had missed part of the first half after being poked in the eye, returned and made six three-point field goals. The lead increased to 31 points late in the third quarter and the Celtics never stopped, upping it to 41 points on Tony Allen's "Alley Oop" shot with 82 seconds to play.

Pierce, who won the Finals MVP trophy, had 17 points and 10 assists while Ray Allen had 26 points, including 7-of-9 three-pointers. Rondo, as noted earlier, was electric with his scoring, play-making, rebounding and defense.

When the final numbers were in, the Celtics' defensive game had proved the old adage to be correct. And despite their two losses to the Lakers, the Celtics were the best team over the entire series and, as noted earlier, punctuated their triumph with a crushing 131-92 victory in the deciding sixth game. Bryant, though the playoffs scoring leader with a 30.6 average, was continually stymied by the defensive skills of Pierce and Allen as Boston's overall physical defensive performance backed down the flashy Lakers at every crucial turn.

The Celtics had returned to the spot they had long considered their birthright—NBA champions. Two days after their triumph, on a warm Thursday in June, the players, coaches, Ainge's front office staff and Grousbeck's fellow owners were "officially" crowned by tens of thousands of adoring fans in a "duck boat" parade through the streets of downtown Boston—a hallmark of the city's sports champions. The Red Sox twice had traversed the route after winning the World Series, most recently at about the time that the Celtics were beginning their 2007-08 championship season.

Shortly before that season began, Rivers had taken Pierce and Garnett on a "duck boat" tour of those same downtown streets. He deliberately chose one that used the same route as the Red Sox's World Series victory parade and told his two key players that he fully intended that the following June they would celebrate their own championship "duck boat" victory parade along that route.

Rivers was right—they did. And it was the grandest trip of their lives.

Above left: *They did it! (L to R): Ray Allen, coach Doc Rivers, Kevin Garnett, General Manager Danny Ainge and team captain Paul Pierce were five of the chief principals who helped the Celtics return to world championship status.*

Above right: *Celtics managing general partner Wyc Grousbeck holds the Celtics' 17th NBA championship banner while riding atop a duck boat during a mammoth victory parade through downtown Boston. The banner joined the previous 16 championship flags in the rafters of Boston's TD Banknorth Garden prior to the opening of the 2008-09 season.*

Celtics Team Records

YEAR-BY-YEAR CELTICS STANDINGS

Year	Won	Lost	Pct.	Div. Fin.	Coach	Playoff Record	Playoff Finish
1946-47	22	38	.367	6	John Russell		DNQ
1947-48	20	28	.417	4	John Russell	1-2	1st Round
1948-49	25	35	.417	5	Augie Julian		DNQ
1949-50	22	46	.324	6	Augie Julian		DNQ
1950-51	39	30	.565	2	Red Auerbach	0-2	1st Round
1951-52	39	27	.591	2	Red Auerbach	1-2	1st Round
1952-53	46	25	.648	3	Red Auerbach	3-3	Conf. Final
1953-54	42	30	.583	2	Red Auerbach	2-4	Conf. Final
1954-55	36	36	.500	3	Red Auerbach	3-4	Conf. Final
1955-56	39	33	.542	2	Red Auerbach	1-2	1st Round
1956-57	44	28	.611	1	Red Auerbach	7-3	NBA Title
1957-58	49	23	.681	1	Red Auerbach	6-5	Div. Title
1958-59	52	22	.722	1	Red Auerbach	8-3	NBA Title
1959-60	59	16	.787	1	Red Auerbach	8-5	NBA Title
1960-61	57	22	.722	1	Red Auerbach	8-2	NBA Title
1961-62	60	20	.750	1	Red Auerbach	8-6	NBA Title
1962-63	58	22	.725	1	Red Auerbach	8-5	NBA Title
1963-64	59	21	.738	1	Red Auerbach	8-2	NBA Title
1964-65	62	18	.755	1	Red Auerbach	8-4	NBA Title
1965-66	54	26	.675	2	Red Auerbach	11-6	NBA Title
1966-67	60	21	.741	2	Bill Russell	4-5	Div. Final
1967-68	54	28	.659	2	Bill Russell	12-7	NBA Title
1968-69	48	34	.585	4	Bill Russell	12-6	NBA Title
1969-70	34	48	.415	6	Tom Heinsohn		DNQ
1970-71	44	38	.537	3	Tom Heinsohn		DNQ
1971-72	56	26	.683	1	Tom Heinsohn	5-6	Conf. Final
1972-73	68	14	.829	1	Tom Heinsohn	7-6	Conf. Final
1973-74	56	26	.683	1	Tom Heinsohn	12-6	NBA Title
1974-75	60	22	.732	1	Tom Heinsohn	6-5	Conf. Final
1975-76	54	28	.659	1	Tom Heinsohn	12-6	NBA Title
1976-77	44	38	.537	2	Tom Heinsohn	5-4	Conf. Final
1977-78	32	50	.390	3	Tom Heinsohn Tom Sanders		DNQ
1978-79	29	53	.354	5	Tom Sanders Dave Cowens		DNQ
1979-80	61	24	.744	1	Bill Fitch	5-4	Conf. Final
1980-81	62	20	.756	1	Bill Fitch	12-5	NBA Title
1981-82	63	19	.768	1	Bill Fitch	7-5	Conf. Final
1982-83	56	26	.683	2	Bill Fitch	2-5	Conf. Semis
1983-84	62	20	.756	1	K.C. Jones	15-8	NBA Title
1984-85	63	19	.768	1	K.C. Jones	13-8	Conf. Title
1985-86	67	15	.817	1	K.C. Jones	15-3	NBA Title
1986-87	59	23	.720	1	K.C. Jones	13-10	Conf. Title
1987-88	57	25	.695	1	K.C. Jones	9-8	Conf. Final
1988-89	42	40	.512	3	Jimmy Rodgers	0-3	1st Round
1989-90	52	30	.634	2	Jimmy Rodgers	2-3	1st Round
1990-91	56	26	.683	1	Chris Ford	5-6	Conf. Semis
1991-92	51	31	.622	1	Chris Ford	6-4	2nd Round
1992-93	48	34	.585	2	Chris Ford	1-3	1st Round
1993-94	32	50	.390	5	Chris Ford		DNQ
1994-95	35	47	.427	3	Chris Ford	1-3	1st Round
1995-96	33	49	.402	5	M.L. Carr		DNQ
1996-97	15	67	.183	7	M.L. Carr		DNQ
1997-98	36	46	.438	6	Rick Pitino		DNQ
1998-99	19	31	.380	5	Rick Pitino		DNQ
1999-00	35	47	.427	5	Rick Pitino		DNQ
2000-01	12	22	.353		Rick Pitino		
	24	24	.500	5	Jim O'Brien		DNQ
2001-02	49	33	.598	2	Jim O'Brien	9-7	Conf. Final
2002-03	44	38	.537	3	Jim O'Brien	4-6	2nd Round
2003-04	22	24	.478		Jim O'Brien		
	14	22	.388	4	John Carroll	0-4	1st Round
2004-05	45	37	.548	1	Doc Rivers	3-4	1st Round
2005-06	33	49	.402	3	Doc Rivers		DNQ
2006-07	24	58	.292	5	Doc Rivers		DNQ
2007-08	66	16	.805	1	Doc Rivers	16-10	NBA Title

ALL-TIME CELTICS CAREER LEADERS

GAMES PLAYED

Player	Years	No.
John Havlicek	1962-78	1270
Robert Parish	1980-94	1106
Kevin McHale	1980-93	971
Bill Russell	1956-69	963
Bob Cousy	1950-63	917

REBOUNDS

Player	Years	No.
Bill Russell	1957-69	21,620
Robert Parish	1980-94	11,051
Dave Cowens	1970-80	10,170
Larry Bird	1979-92	8,974
John Havlicek	1962-78	8,007

POINTS

Player	Years	No.
John Havlicek	1962-78	26,395
Larry Bird	1979-92	21,791
Robert Parish	1980-94	18,245
Kevin McHale	1980-93	17,335
Bob Cousy	1950-63	16,955

ASSISTS

Player	Years	No.
Bob Cousy	1950-63	6,949
John Havlicek	1962-78	6,114
Larry Bird	1979-92	5,695
Bill Russell	1956-69	4,100
Jo-Jo White	1969-79	3,686

Below: *Robert Parish was the oldest player in the NBA by the time he retired in 1994. He exemplified the drive and spirit that saw the Celtics win so many NBA championships.*

Index

Page numbers in *italics*
indicate illustrations